Cultivate

Dedication

I thank my bride, Amanda, for sacrificing our time together to do the Lord's work.

Table of Contents

Purpose Statement

Why cultivate? Cultivate is a verb meaning to develop a skill, in this case ministry. Cultivate also means to prepare the soil, in this case preparing the hearts or minds of people. The Bible says, "Does he who plows for sowing plow continually? Does he continually open and harrow his ground?" (Isaiah 28:24). When farmers plow or cultivate the ground, how should they do it? When Christians cultivate the spirits and minds of people, how should we do it?

We should open the hearts of people carefully and purposely to plant the word of God effectively. I pray that this book will help you become a more well-rounded Christian and preacher, to better equip you to lead more people to Christ than you've ever imagined.

This book covers three sections: cultivate the preacher, cultivate the congregation, and cultivate the community. I will share evangelism ideas, spiritual growth ideas, and discipleship ideas. Further, I am sharing sermon ideas with you. Some of these sermons were completely original. By original I mean that I did not consult commentaries, nor did anyone give me an idea. Some of these sermons are ideas generated from life. Some of these sermons I have heard or seen but rearranged to work better in my mind for delivery purposes. You may notice that some sermons are familiar to you, even If I claim that they are original to me. Rightfully so, when one reads the Bible and studies the scriptures carefully and accurately, they will certainly have similar sermons when compared to other preachers who also study the scriptures with accuracy.

As surely as there is oxygen in the air, preachers in America, Kenya and Haiti are using this book in their national language on the mission field right now.

May God bless your every effort!

"How beautiful upon the mountains are the feet of him who brings good news, who publishes peace, who brings good news of happiness, who publishes salvation, who says to Zion 'Your God reigns' (Isaiah 52:7).

--- **Chad Garrett**

Chapter 1

Cultivate the Preacher

A dynamic preacher

A dynamic preacher is multi-talented, deep thinking, charismatic, and loving, yet firm on the truth. Preaching is only one-fifth of what makes a dynamic preacher. Just like a great football player, he must be in good physical condition, he must know the game, he must be a leader, he must be able to use the ball well, and he must improve. "And Jesus increased in wisdom and in stature and in favor with God and man" (Luke 2:52). Notice Jesus improved in His knowledge (intellectual component). He improved in His stature (maturity component). He improved in His relationship with God (spiritual component). Jesus improved in favor with people (relationship/fellowship/leadership component).

Five components of a dynamic preacher:

1. Wisdom/Knowledge (knows/understands God's word)
2. Maturity (physical health and mental maturity that comes with age)
3. Loves God (commitment to God)
4. Loves people and can lead people (personal evangelism and leadership)
5. Preaches well

A preacher can and should improve in all these areas as he continues serving the Lord. After all, Jesus did and we are to be imitators of Him.

SPIRITUAL CONDITION

How can we assess our spiritual condition? The spiritual state of the preacher is the most important aspect of being a preacher. Ask yourself:

- "Why am I a preacher?"
- "How close am I to God right now?"
- "Am I living a truthful, faithful and honest life?"
- "How is my relationship with my wife?"
- "Am I growing, learning, and practicing Christianity more every year?"

Preachers must examine their spiritual condition constantly.

"Not many of you should become teachers, my brothers, for you know that we who teach will be judged with greater strictness. For we all stumble in many ways. And if anyone does not stumble in what he says, he is a perfect man, able also to bridle his whole body" (James 3:1-2). Some preachers are preachers because it is a job and a way for them to make money. Some preachers preach because they can gain fame and popularity or control over people. Examine yourself and ask, "Why am I preaching"? The spiritual state of a man is the most important aspect of being a dynamic preacher.

To become more spiritual and grow closer to God, you need to pray every day and put the principles of God's word into action. You need to surround yourself with one or two other respectable men who can be mentors and who will give you advice.

Finally, why is your relationship with your wife listed? The Bible says, "Likewise, husbands, live with your wives in an understanding way, showing honor to the woman as the weaker vessel, since they are heirs with you of the grace of life, so that your prayers may not be hindered" (1 Peter 3:7). So, how are you treating your wife?

LOVES AND KNOWS PEOPLE

Ask yourself, "How am I treating people? How do the people around me define my reputation?"

Be careful not to let the opinion of everyone else define you, but the community at large should think of you positively, having respect both for you and your work. Not because you support them financially. Not because you cater to their every need. They should have respect for you because you listen to them and pray for them. The community should have respect for you because you stand firm on the word of God and live it! The Bible says that we should come to the house of the Lord so that, "He may teach us His ways and that we may walk in His paths" (Isaiah 2:3). The community should see you walking righteously while struggling physically or emotionally with them.

The same is true for the congregation. The congregation must respect you, trust you, and see that you care about them. Do not be afraid to show them that even you struggle in this life trying to carry your burdens and theirs. When people expect money or things from you and you cannot help them in that way, talk with them privately and pray with them. Do not ignore them or avoid them.

Loving people can be difficult. That is because some people have a hard time getting along with others. However, there is always an explanation of why people act the way they do. Perhaps there's been some childhood trauma or abuse or a lot of emotional pain in that person's life. Some people make it difficult to love them but really do need love.

As a preacher, you are in the people business. Think of how the Israelites rebelled against God and were disobedient. Think about how they were influenced by Egyptian idolatry from their past. Even though the Egyptians abused them, they still carried with them Egyptian influences. Moses was a man who dealt with people and their problems and even pleaded to God on behalf of the people.

Your business is to deal with people all the time. The same is true for elders, deacons and all Christians! "For you were called to freedom, brothers. Only do not use your freedom as an opportunity for the flesh, but through love serve one another. For the whole law is fulfilled in one word: 'You shall love your neighbor as yourself.' But if you bite and devour one another, watch out that you are not consumed by one another" (Galatians 5:13-15). "Brothers, if anyone is caught in any transgression, you who are spiritual should restore him in a spirit of gentleness. Keep watch on yourself, lest you too be tempted. Bear on another's burdens, and so fulfill the law of Christ" (Galatians 6:1-2). You must love people and plead to God for their souls. Pray for everyone and show them you love them by spending time with them.

PERSONAL EVANGELISM

Personal evangelism happens in small settings. I know it looks glorious to preach to hundreds of people and see many baptized, but personal evangelism doesn't happen in front of hundreds of people. Personal evangelism happens in small groups or in one-on-one Bible studies. This is an opportunity for the prospect (the person you are studying with) to read the Bible for themselves and believe in the words of God. Small settings are where discipleship takes place because the environment allows people to feel comfortable enough to ask questions and talk about life. You will also be able to develop a better relationship with people in smaller groups.

There are a few barriers to evangelism such as inexperience, nervousness, and one-way communication. Some preachers are not experienced in personal Bible studies. I have seen preachers who have been preaching for years and do great preaching to hundreds of people in Gospel meetings. However, they are not sure what to do in smaller more personal settings. Further, some preachers or Christians are too nervous to start a personal study or conduct a study with a prospect.

Most preachers and Christians know many scriptures but do not know where to start or what scriptures to use at the right time. Sometimes people want to tell the prospect what to do instead of letting the prospect read the scriptures. The prospect must be given the opportunity of understanding what the word of God means, on their own. The Bible study helper should do as little talking as possible during a Bible study. There is a simple process to follow that works. The area of personal evangelism is so important, I have written an entire chapter on it (see Cultivate the Community).

LEAD PEOPLE

How are Christians supposed to lead people? We need to look at Christ. He leads us from the front. He is challenging us because He has done more than we can do. He is doing more than anyone of us could fathom. We need to lead people from the front by getting our hands dirty, working hard, and breaking a sweat. We need to be on the ground with people and there is no task that we are "too good" to do. Many people think they can just show up Sunday, teach, preach, and share their knowledge with people and be satisfied. That is not enough. Leadership is not made in an office behind closed doors. Nor is leadership demonstrated by standing up and speaking up (one time each week). Leadership happens with the people throughout the week.

Naomi was a leader for Ruth. Ruth was convicted to say, "For, where you go I will go, and where you lodge I will lodge. Your people shall be my people, and your God my God" (Ruth 1:16). Imagine if the people in your community felt the same way about you. Imagine if they told you "Where you will go I will go." What if they said, "Your God will be my God"? What was it that Naomi did as a leader? She was in a tragic situation, yet she had a plan that was founded on God and she took action!

You can do this. Be imitators of Christ (1 Corinthians 11:1). One of my favorite conversations was the one Jesus led in John chapter 4. Jesus personally taught a Samaritan woman. Samaritans had a terrible reputation, but Jesus loved them. Jesus stayed with the people for a couple of days. Then, Jesus reminds His disciples to preach the gospel in Samaria in Acts 1:8. It is no wonder that so many Samaritans believed and were baptized in Acts 8! Jesus laid the groundwork of loving and leading people to God. Be imitators of him.

PREACHING WELL

Though preachers think that preaching well is the most important part of their job, it is not. How can a preacher preach well if he is spiritually corrupt? How can a preacher preach well if no one will listen to him because of his reputation? However, preaching is still very important, so I will address how to do it the best way possible. In the chapters ahead, I will be going over sermon design and delivery, and providing a number of sermon outlines. Preachers are public speakers and need to understand how to communicate, as well as how to design a sermon.

Cultivate means to acquire a skill, so let us finish talking about preachers acquiring skills to become great! There are a few things he must do. First, great preachers are not made quickly. Let's all remember that. We need to have a long-term mindset and allow the Lord and our brothers and sisters to help us mature through the years to become dynamic preachers. There are a few things that need our attention, lest we lose focus, or fail to reach the goal of becoming great.

Many preachers get burned out, or exhausted, and quit. Some preachers become discouraged by negative things said to them from the community, churches or church leaders. Some preachers spend more time with the church and the church members causing their families to become resentful of the church. Some preachers fall prey to the love of money, fame, lust, adultery and even alcohol/drugs. Some preachers leave the church to become denominational preachers. Most young preachers would deny that any of these things could happen to them, but history tells us over and over that they do. So, what can we do as preachers to guard against such catastrophes and ambushes the devil has set for us?

We need mentors, we need friends, and we need to pace ourselves with a long-term approach to preaching and we need to keep God first, wife and children next, then church members and people in the community. We will discuss all of these areas in this chapter.

Mentorship

"Iron sharpens iron, and one man sharpens another" (Proverbs 27:17).

Preachers "sharpen" each other through fellowship. Preachers need to get together and pray for each other. They need to have seminars and gospel meetings together. They need to build great friendships and teamwork. In many places of the world, preachers have felt they have a territory or an area that belongs to them and do not want other preachers working in their area. However, the Bible says, "Two are better than one, because they have a good reward for their toil. For if they fall, one will lift up his fellow. But woe to him who is alone when he falls and has not another to lift him up!" (Ecclesiastes 4:9-10).

One of David Pharr's greatest contributions to preachers and men in North and South Carolina is "Men's Day". "Men's Day" takes place on a Saturday where several men take turns delivering short sermon lessons, with several songs sung in between. A fellowship lunch is provided for all who come. It is a time of great fellowship and encouragement. Men's Day has grown over the years to six hundred men in attendance. That tells you how people have received such an opportunity. That tells you how badly we need to meet together as men, as leaders, and as preachers to encourage one another. Think about how you can start a men's day to get people together to encourage one another.

When preachers come together they should share sermons, sermon outlines or ideas. Some preachers think that when they design a sermon, they must protect it and not let people know about it or ask people to give them credit for it. I mentioned in the purpose statement of this book that the Bible is God's word. While I appreciate the way in which preachers have crafted their sermons, we need to be more concerned about educating and encouraging our fellow preachers by sharing our ideas.

Sharing your ideas, sharing your sermons, and using other people's ideas or sermons will only help you become more well-rounded in your abilities. You will become a better, more dynamic speaker. However, sharing sermons does not mean copying word for word and even mimicking the exact behavior of another preacher. Sermons should be studied, tailored for your use, and delivered in the most effective way to help the audience. Audiences or congregations face different challenges, causing them to need different sermons to speak to their circumstances. You will need to make changes to these sermons I have shared with you to be more meaningful to your congregation.

Everyone needs a mentor. A mentor will help you become better than you are right now. The first step to finding a mentor is allowing yourself to be mentored. You have to humble yourself and accept teaching and correction. You must become a student of the Bible who asks questions and is ready to make changes personally. Sometimes it is tough to be corrected, especially when you think you are doing things right.

When you think of a mentor, think of someone with great wisdom. What is wisdom? Wisdom is more than knowledge. Wisdom is more than skills. Wisdom comes from a working knowledge through life resulting in skills and experience. While there are some younger men with more wisdom than older men, most of the time mentors are at least fifteen years older than those being mentored. Older people have experience and have acquired skills resulting in wisdom.

Solomon spent most of the book of Ecclesiastes telling us to cherish wisdom. We need to cherish wisdom and our mentors who share their wisdom. Remember, mentors do not ask to be such, they are asked to do it. So, you need to ask men to mentor you. This takes great humility, but is truly necessary. Please find someone who is a good mentor to talk to and help you become great.

Personally, I have several mentors who are different from one another to help me grow in many ways. If someone does not want to mentor, move on, they should not mentor you if they do not want to. People who are good mentors want to mentor. Actually, coming to men asking them to mentor you is a great compliment and gives them fulfillment. Good mentors enjoy mentoring. I have had some of my mentors tell me "Thank you." However, they know how grateful I am for their valuable time and guidance.

Setting Goals

The preacher needs to have goals written down. Write down the big picture plan or goals you would like to achieve in five years. Then write down yearly goals, followed by monthly goals. The Bible says "The toil of a fool wearies him, for he does not know the way to the city" (Ecclesiastes 10:15). Solomon also tells us, "The wise person has his eyes in his head, but the fool walks in darkness." (Ecclesiastes 2:14a). He also says "Better is the sight of the eyes than the wandering of the appetite: this also is vanity and a striving after wind" (Ecclesiastes 6:9). Look at where you are going! If you do not have a target to aim for, you'll never get there. So, write down your plans and goals so that you can see clearly where you are going.

However, with all plans, write them in pencil, because God may have something different in mind. What I mean is, be flexible. Remember, setting goals helps you improve as a minister and as a Christian. A preacher's purpose for his ministry should not be about personal gain (1 Timothy 6:5). Here is the point, stay on task, and accomplish your goals. "As for you, always be sober-minded, endure suffering, do the work of an evangelist, fulfill your ministry" (2 Timothy 4:5). The Bible says,

"Look carefully then how you walk, not as unwise but as wise, making the best use of the time, because the days are evil. Therefore, do not be foolish, but understand what the will of the Lord is" (Ephesians 5:15-17).

What are you setting goals for exactly? Set personal goals for developing as a preacher and as a Christian. Set goals for developing several different sermon topics throughout the year. The congregation you lead will grow when they read and understand God's word as a whole. The Bible says, "Therefore I intend always to remind you of these qualities, though you know them and are established in the truth that you have" (2 Peter 1:12). We do need to remind people of teachings they already know, but we also need to teach all of God's word by covering many different topics.

Think about the Lord's congregation and set goals to help them grow into leaders, song leaders and elders. You can do this by teaching them to develop lessons, teach classes, or teach about the Lord's communion. You can also practice singing with them to develop song leaders. Teach others to be teachers and preachers. Great leaders ask themselves "who is going to take my place?" Great leaders find the future leaders of tomorrow and help them mature as leaders.

Finally, set goals for evangelism and campaign work. When you set goals for campaign work, invite and include other preachers and church members from churches of Christ near you, to help the Lord's congregation that you serve. This helps people in the community see the fellowship and strength of the congregations.

Set goals:
- Personal growth
- Sermons that need to be taught
- Growing the congregation
- Finding and teaching song leaders
- Developing new preachers
- Establishing leadership (elders & deacons)
- Campaigns

Strive for Eldership

Every young man should strive to be an elder in the church. The qualifications for elders laid out in 1 Timothy 3:1-7 and Titus 1:5-9 are really qualifications that all godly, Christian men should have. Becoming an elder is like planting trees. They should have been planted 30 years ago or more. Eldership training must start early because qualifications for an elder takes years to achieve. They must have a sound, faithful family and they must have a great reputation.

Naturally, some men are this way coming into the faith and develop quickly as men of God and become elders. Most people think we must start teaching older men how to be elders in the church. We do need to teach older men right now. In addition, we need to instill the desire to be an elder in our young people. We must show our elders honor and respect so that young men will see their importance and significance in the church.

Elders are also known as shepherds. Shepherds should be visiting the people and praying with the people and teaching the people so the people learn to love and appreciate them. The elders should even tend to the young people. Peter was an elder and shepherd of the church. Jesus told Peter to "Feed my sheep" and "Tend to my sheep" in John 21:16-17. These passages show us that elders should be with the people; leading them, and feeding them spiritually.

The qualifications of an elder largely rests on an individual's purity and commitment to God. However, his family partially qualifies him to be an elder, which is why he must take care of his family along the way. If he is constantly putting other people before his family, his family may come to resent the church and may even resent him. Elders should make sure they are present for their family (birthdays, special occasions, etc.). Remember, God first, then your spouse, and your children.

In places like Kenya or in Haiti, many congregations do not have elders because the preacher wants to be the "pastor". Preachers are not "pastors" unless they also serve as an elder with at least one more elder. The word "elder" is simply another word for "pastor" and there must always be a plurality of them. In Titus 1:5, the word "elders" is plural, meaning more than one. You will also notice in the same passage that there should be elders at every congregation or every town.

Many times, preachers don't want elders because they do not want someone overseeing them because the preacher wants to be in control. This is not God's will. Many congregations do not have elderships because people in the congregation are underdeveloped spiritually. Raising the level of spiritual knowledge and spiritual maturity of the whole congregation will develop elders from within the congregation.

Deacons are not only servants, but they are the work horses of the congregation. The qualifications for deacons are found in 1 Timothy 3:8. When a congregation has committed deacons who are given the autonomy to get the job done, great things happen for the Lord. Let us pray that every congregation will have elders and deacons that are working hard for the Lord!

CHAPTER 2

Cultivate the Congregation

Strong congregations have not only Biblically-qualified leaders but also members who are strongly committed to discipleship. The word "disciple" is used to designate someone who wants to learn something and practice it. In this case, a disciple is someone who wants to learn about Jesus Christ and practice Christianity. Therefore, discipleship is assisting people to learn Christianity and practice it.

Please understand that assisting someone to be a Christian does not mean paying them money. Assisting someone who wants to grow as a Christian may be spending time with them, reading the Bible together, praying together, and showing them how to preach or conduct a Bible study or how to deal with challenging situations. In this chapter, we will consider two important questions:

- **What does "Cultivate your Congregation" mean?**
- **How do you do it?**

Cultivate means to acquire a skill. So, we must seek to help church members acquire the skills needed to become a more committed and better disciple, while ministering to one another and the community. To become ministers, we must be disciples.

So, how are we going to disciple the church? Discipleship happens very little from the pulpit, or from open air meetings or Gospel meetings. Many preachers believe they can show up, stand up (on Sunday), speak up, and sit down, and they are done with the congregation for the week. In contrast, Jesus discipled the apostles as they walked through Samaria (John 4) and other places in practical settings (Matthew chapters 5-9) that almost always involved other people. Jesus also discipled the apostles in small groups and quiet places. Jesus Christ and apostle Paul taught us that teaching other people to mature in Christ (discipleship) is most effective in small group settings or even one-on-one settings.

What I am talking about is helping Christians in your congregation increase in their knowledge and their ability to teach, preach, Bible study, pray, sing, carry out benevolence to others around them, and teach outsiders about Christ. All Christians should be striving in discipleship to grow and improve.

How can Christians grow if they are not discipling one another? Sometimes preachers do not want members of the congregation to grow because the preacher feels threatened. Preachers may feel like they could lose their position to someone else, so they do not want elders to lead the church or to develop other Christian men to become preachers. This is a power struggle and it is not a Biblical concept. On the contrary, we need to develop Christian leaders who will one day take our place. We need to plant new congregations. These new congregations will need preachers, song leaders, elders and deacons. So, churches need to develop leaders and preachers from within.

There are only twenty-four hours in one day. There are only seven days in a week. Therefore, the preacher needs to manage his time well and needs to spend time meeting with church members in small groups to disciple them. Many people would be very encouraged to have the opportunity to grow and learn from their preachers.

WHY DEVELOP LEADERS?

If we are going to be disciples and make disciples we must follow God's word! "This is why I left you in Crete, so that you might put what remained into order, and appoint elders in every town as I directed you" (Titus 1:5).

Further, the Bible says, "and what you have heard from me in the presence of many witnesses entrust to faithful men who will be able to teach others also" (2 Timothy 2:2). Preachers need to develop leaders within the congregation to do the work and share in the work load of the church.

"For just as the body is one and has many members, and all the members of the body, though many, are one body, so it is with Christ" (1 Corinthians 12:12). The church is made of many different people. Men, women, young people and children. All of these individuals have different abilities and interests. The Bible encourages us to work together using the different abilities and talents we have.

Discipleship must include helping people find their abilities and use them for the Lord. We must meet with people and talk to them about what they want to do for the Lord. The work of the Church is exciting and is alive. Give other people a taste of it and they will want to be a part of it.

However, there are struggles with this in different cultures. Some people do not want to share knowledge, or they expect to be paid if they do something for the church. The Bible says, "But godliness with contentment is great gain, for we brought nothing into the world, and we cannot take anything out of the world. But if we have food and clothing, with these we will be content" (1 Timothy 6:6-8). I understand there are certain things people cannot do because they do not have the resources. However, having a Bible study with someone, leading songs for the congregation during worship, leading prayer for the congregation during worship, and teaching about the Lord's communion are things that all Christian men should strive to do.

Further, we must live a Christian lifestyle free from the love of money, and abstain from drunkenness. Living a moral life for Christ does not entitle us to receive money. I pray we can be Christians for free, trusting in Christ and following him.

What about preachers? Preachers do need support if they are going to work as preachers. The Bible supports this concept of supporting the local preacher (see 1 Corinthians 9). However, many preachers will also have to work to support themselves like Paul did and I do.

DEVELOP DISCIPLES

The first thing we must do when meeting with people is teach them sound doctrine. The word "doctrine" means teaching. Teach the truth. Teach disciples how to study the Bible and understand how important teaching the truth is. We must all develop a love for the truth so that we can live a strong, faithful and joyful life before God. We must develop a love for the truth so we can recognize and correct false teaching.

Think about this; if a child gets fed candy every day, the child will like the candy. When it is time to eat a meal, the child does not want real food, but wants the candy. We know that candy is not good for our teeth and cannot sustain us. This is how we must approach the truth. The truth is meat and rice. False teaching is candy. We must develop a love and respect for meat and rice (the truth) which will sustain us and not the candy (false teaching) which hurts us.

Where do we start when discipling people? Start by teaching and reading the truth. "Sanctify them in truth; your word is truth" (John 17:17). Jesus wants us to be set apart and completely committed to His truth. Seeking, reading and teaching the truth is the first step in discipleship.

Commitment is the second step in discipleship. Commitment means to be dedicated to or to feel an obligation to something. We must be committed to God, Jesus Christ and the Holy Spirit. We must be committed to the word of God and to growing together with Christian brothers or sisters.

Finally, we must be committed to teaching others (outside the church). The teacher must be committed and the one being taught must be committed to the mission of Christianity which is saving souls and living a faithful life. People will believe in the truth, but the amount of people committed to the truth (seeking and teaching) are few. Truth comes first, followed by commitment to the truth. One cannot expect to grow without commitment.

There certainly needs to be a relationship between those who are discipling and those who are being discipled. This relationship needs to be founded on the great mission of being a Christian and following God together. Saving souls should be second only to teaching the truth for new converts. We must instill within the new converts and those who are mature in the faith, the idea of soul winning for Jesus. Self-propagation, that is to grow the number of people in the local congregation, begins with a mindset of evangelism.

If you give people too much work, they may quit. If you do not give them anything to do, they will go somewhere else to find something meaningful to be a part of. Building relationships is mentoring. Mentoring is like parenting. Parents start off as disciplinarians and teachers. After their children have grown to adults, parents are no longer disciplinarians. They have the opportunity to be friends and give advice when asked. These mentor/parent like relationships are what we need in the church to help us grow.

SEED SOWERS

I recently started a Bible class entitled "Seed Sowers." Our purpose is to meet together and conquer very practical work for the Lord. We want to do Bible studies with people and are doing everything we can to find contacts or start Bible studies. So, I assign participants in the class to contact members who have gone wayward and ask them for prayer requests. I assign people to call church members and their families for encouragement. We can only get Bible studies when we start talking to people.

What do you do when you contact people? Call people or visit people for prayers and share scriptures or read scriptures together. Ask questions and look in the Bible for answers. We would ask everyone we called if there was someone we could Bible study with or a contact they could give us to call. We especially called people who were recently baptized to find out who they know that might be interested in a Bible study. Think about it, a newly baptized person is highly motivated to share their testimony and has a new (possibly unreached) circle of friends and family. Please remember this, before you start a Bible study, you should have a Bible study plan and be prepared to execute the plan (more on this later).

When leading campaigns, make sure to get members of the Lord's congregation involved. Give them important work to do. Printing advertisements, personally inviting people, praying, singing, preaching, and setting up the facilities are all necessary for conducting a campaign.

Further, women seminars are really helpful for women. Women need to teach women how to conduct seminars for women only. That means the women do the teaching, praying and singing, because men are absent. When American women come to Africa to conduct a seminar for women, I ask one or two women locally to translate. The local women learn how to do the seminar while translating and are better prepared to conduct their own the next time. It's important to encourage different women to grow in their abilities to translate and conduct seminars for women.

CONGREGATIONS IN THE BIBLE

The Bible is very clear how a congregation should operate. There are three major components that all congregations should have.

1. Self-governing

2. Self-propagating

3. Self-supporting

Self-governing and self-propagating are the most important concepts here. A congregation led by the local people (hopefully having elders and deacons) is a congregation that should be able to govern itself. After establishing leadership from within the congregation, the leadership must decide on difficult issues and even discipline members for living unfaithfully.

Discipline may come out in the form of urging people to repent publicly and praying with them or talking to them about it. For instance, congregations in Kenya or in Haiti need to be functioning on their own, not relying on American leadership to function. I am not talking about money, but about teaching, preaching, leadership, and discipline.

How long did Paul stay at congregations he started? Paul did not stay at a congregation for five years, so why do Americans? I pray that my American brothers and sisters will start congregations and get out of the way. Missionaries should be pioneers, planting new congregations and teaching people the right way to study the Bible and preach. Unfortunately, when missionaries work with a congregation continuously for years and years, the ability of the local people to take over the work decreases. Nationals get frustrated or discouraged to lead because Americans are telling them (by their unwillingness to leave) that the nationals are not good enough to lead.

Every congregation must be self-propagating. The reason Jesus Christ died on the cross was for people to believe in Him and be saved by the Gospel. We need to bleed with conviction about the cross and remember the redeeming sacrifice for us and share it with others. Evangelism is contagious, so let's get everyone in the congregation to reach out to others. Without self-propagation, the congregation will die.

I pray that the Christians in Kenya and Haiti will teach their neighbors and their community through personal Bible studies or small group Bible studies. However, in Kenya and in Haiti most nationals want to do crusades or campaigns where they have a big open-air meeting. This can be helpful, but is usually expected to be paid for by Americans, which is not the right answer. The nationals can support their own crusades or open-air meetings. It may take them a year to save up the money to do that, but they can do it on their own.

Finally, there is the self-supporting congregation. Congregations should be self-supporting. They should not be supported by foreign money. When a congregation supports its own preacher, they have a closer connection with the preacher. When the congregation builds its own buildings, the people will take better care of the building and have real ownership of their faith they can see. When a congregation supports itself, giving increases. Giving is worship. When foreign money provides everything nationals need, giving (worship) from the nationals decreases and so does personal responsibility.

Many congregations around the world depend on American churches or an American missionary to tell them what to do or support them financially. The Bible tells us the new/young congregations that Paul started gave money to help the stronger/older congregation in Jerusalem. This is exactly opposite of what we are doing today. Please pray to God that He will help you and the congregation you are a part of to thrive locally.

Sometimes things look nicer with money and things get done faster with money, but typically, when the money runs out so do the nice things and the amount of work decreases. However, with faith and commitment, longer, slower, but attainable goals are reached when God is the One we depend on. There are real struggles for our brothers and sisters and life is tough, almost unbearable for many Christians. That is what faith is all about, to get us through life, to give us the push. Though money runs out, love does not. "So now faith, hope, and love abide, these three; but the greatest of these is love" (1 Corinthians 13:13). Let us depend on God, not money.

STUDYING THE BIBLE

Many times, people will say comments such as "the Bible can be interpreted many different ways" or "you have your interpretation of a scripture and I have mine". What people really are saying is that the Bible can be made to say what we want it to say. They may go so far as to say the Bible is just written by men with different opinions. All of these claims are false. "All Scripture is breathed out by God and profitable for teaching, for reproof, for correction, and for training in righteousness, that the man of God may be competent, equipped for every good work" (2 Timothy 3:16-17).

The Bible is God's word and will not contradict itself (1 Corinthians 14:33). The Bible should not be used to confirm how we want to live. Scriptures do not change and adapt to our life. Instead, the Bible points us in the right direction. We must approach the Bible with a willing heart to change our lives to follow the scriptures.

The Bible certainly helps us in different ways throughout our life. When we are struggling with grief, the Psalms may be more meaningful and helpful. Perhaps we have a lot of stress and the Epistles offer us hope, or we are wandering from the truth and the book of Acts brings us restoration or back to New Testament teachings.

There are many times we read the Bible and new words or new verses are understood better. All of these "new things" are evidence that our knowledge is growing, which is good. It is not considered different interpretations. The word interpretation means "to derive meaning". So, to say a verse has different interpretations means the verse has different meanings. This could only be true with dual prophecy scriptures or figurative language and there are a few of those scriptures.

On the other hand, the majority of the Bible consists of scriptures that mean what they mean... literally. This is certainly the case when it comes to becoming a Christian and worshiping God correctly. The Bible means what it means and we must apply the right meaning to our lives today.

We need help when studying the Bible to stay in the right context. When we examine scripture, we need to ask:

- What covenant is the verse under (New or Old)?

- Who wrote it (author)?

- When was it written (time frame and historical events of the time)?

- Why was it written (look for the purpose statement of the book or chapter)?

- Read the whole book, read the whole chapter surrounding the verse.

- When we have the right context, we can derive the right meaning from the verse.

SERVANT LEADERSHIP

I would regret not mentioning the terms "servant leadership". A servant makes sacrifices and carries burdens to ensure a job gets done. Jesus was a servant as He died for our sins. Leadership is the ability to achieve a high standard causing other people to want to follow you.

Sometimes preachers will graduate preaching schools and think they are too good for certain jobs. Has Jesus ever had that attitude? We need servant evangelists, servant teachers, and servant leadership to disciple the congregations of the Lord's church. Leadership is nothing without service. Evangelism cannot happen if preachers or Christians think they are too good for evangelism.

When was the last time you went to someone's home to visit them, pray with them and see what is in their hearts (hoping they are ready for salvation)? Let us surround "cultivate the congregation" with prayer. After all, we are serving God who answers prayers. Be a servant leader who prays and God will bless you as you go.

CHAPTER 3

Cultivate the Community

Cultivating the community means reaching out to people outside of the church through campaigns, Bible studies, benevolence, and friendships to acquire new Christians in the faith. Just as a farmer prepares the ground, so the soil will receive the seed and grow into a plentiful harvest, so Christians must cultivate the soil (minds) of people so they will receive the word of God and grow strong in the faith. People need to know you care about them and when they believe you care about them, they will listen to you.

Now, let us talk about benevolence. Benevolence means bestowing goodness and kindness to someone else while expecting nothing in return and it is a crucial component of church work. Let us pray that every outreach opportunity will end up in a Bible study. The rest of this chapter is about cultivating Bible studies and specifically focuses on personal relationships in smaller groups or one on one with people.

Whether you use materials, study guides, or just the Bible, I would challenge anyone who denies that the Bible does not teach a method of studying the Gospel with someone. In the first few chapters of the book of Acts, the apostles preached the Gospel. They reminded us that Jesus was attested to by signs, that he was unfairly killed, and that God raised him from the dead.

Developing Interest

People are fascinating! I have a natural tendency to be interested in what people are doing and like to talk about it. That goes a long way when you are trying to develop friendships with people. In an effort to develop relationships, I went to Nyansakia for a crusade and spent the morning hours visiting people in the fields and in their homes. Many people came for at least one of the Gospel meeting nights.

My favorite interaction was at a high school. I asked one of the church members in his twenties to gather his friends, I bought a soccer ball and we went to the high school to play the high school team. After the game, I prayed with the young men and talked to them about being strong, godly men. I shared scriptures and invited them to the crusade. One of their teachers was there and was very thankful for a good message. Those young men listened to me because I played my heart out with them. Get out there with the people and you will make a difference for the Lord and in the lives of the community.

For the purpose of this book, I will refer to people I want to study the Bible with as "prospects." Developing a prospect's interest is your job as God's servant. You must find creative ways to get people's attention and turn that attention into Bible studies. Try asking open ended questions like, "How many people will be saved?" or "Why are there so many different churches?" Then, allow them to answer the question. Then ask, "Let's see what the Bible says about that. When can we meet again Tuesday or Thursday, which?" Set the appointment and start the study!

The Method

Look at the following passages, and let's consider the method the disciples used.

"Men of Israel, hear these words. Jesus of Nazareth, a man attested to you by God with mighty works and wonders and signs that God did through him in your midst, as you yourselves know—this Jesus, delivered up according to the definite plan and foreknowledge of God, you crucified and killed by the hands of lawless men. God raised him up, loosing the pangs of death, because it was not possible for him to be held by it." (Acts 2:22–24)

Peter presented the Gospel the same way we need to present the Gospel today. First, Peter established or confirmed the authority of God to people who already believed in God. He reminded them that Jesus's authority was attested by God through signs and wonders.

Second, Peter reminded them of their sin. Every person must understand their sinful state before God. This may be an uncomfortable process, but must take place before a real need for Jesus can even be fathomed.

Third, though they sinned, God made a remedy for their sins which is the third point of this method.

Fourth, conviction brewed in the hearts of the people that clearly saw the reality of their state before almighty God, which caused an immediate response (the fourth point). The people wanted to know what they were to do.

Therefore, Peter called them to action. "And Peter said to them, 'Repent and be baptized every one of you in the name of Jesus Christ for the forgiveness of your sins, and you will receive the gift of the Holy Spirit" (Acts 2:38). Peter continued with the same formula in the following passages from Acts chapter 3 and 4:

"The God of Abraham, the God of Isaac, and the God of Jacob, the God of our fathers, glorified his servant Jesus whom you delivered over and denied in the presence of Pilate, when he had decided to release him. But you denied the Holy and Righteous One, and asked for a murderer to be granted to you, and you killed the Author of life, whom God raised from the dead. To this we are witnesses. . . Repent therefore, and turn back, that your sins may be blotted out" (Acts 3:13–15, 19)

"But many of those who had heard the word believed, and the number of the men came to about five thousand." (Acts 4:4)

"If we are being examined today concerning a good deed done to a crippled man, by what means this man has been healed, let it be known to all of you and to all the people of Israel that by the name of Jesus Christ of Nazareth, whom you crucified, whom God raised from the dead— by him this man is standing before you well. This Jesus is the stone that was rejected by you, the builders, which has become the cornerstone. And there is salvation in no one else, for there is no other name under heaven given among men by which we must be saved." (Acts 4:9–12)

This methodology continued through early Christianity as evidence by the conversions documented in the book of Acts. Consider the account of the Ethiopian eunuch. Philip was sent to the Ethiopian eunuch to help him study the scriptures. They were reading from Isaiah 53, where the eunuch learned about Jesus (God's authority), and that the sacrifice of Jesus was for the sins of the people.

Philip preached to the Ethiopian eunuch the "good news" (Acts 8:35), which is that God made a remedy for our sins through Jesus Christ. The Ethiopian proved his understanding by his response. "And as they were going along the road they came to some water, and the eunuch said, 'See, here is water! What prevents me from being baptized?'" (Acts 8:36).

He responded out of obedience to God when he believed in God and was baptized. The Bible says the Ethiopian went on his way rejoicing! He knew the debt of his sin was paid. Even Paul witnessed the authority and power of Jesus in Acts 9 and went blind. Paul also was made aware of his sin of persecuting Christ and responded by obedience (Acts 22:16).

There are four points and a call to action in all these passages that prove the methodology of Bible study in sequential order:

1. God's authority;
2. We are sinners;
3. God made a remedy; and
4. A call to action.

By the end of a Bible study with someone, these four areas should be understood very clearly by every prospect. Whether obedience to God's will is followed, I believe when the Gospel is heard, the soul is reaching for redemption. God put "eternity" in our hearts, and we know deep down in our soul, that are going somewhere after death. (Ecclesiastes 3:11)

The Process

Being a good example is not enough. Good intentions alone are not going to cut it, nor are poor Bible study techniques. People who have been well-versed for several decades fall prey to a counterproductive way to study the Bible with people. I have taken many people with me to Bible studies, and I see the same thing over and over again. We are too quick to tell people what the Bible says. We are excited and see the pattern of sound words Jesus designed for us to find and obey. We want others to just see it. This approach totally ruins a study. The less we are teaching in a study the better. The less we teach in a study, the more God teaches.

All Bible studies should begin by developing a relationship with the prospect. Start every Bible study with prayer. Next, introduce the study guide to the prospect and explain to them how the study guide works. Then, we must establish God's authority and the Bible as His inspired word. One way to do this is to have the prospect read the scriptures out loud. We should avoid reading the scriptures for them. The scriptures are what change a person's heart.

"For the word of God is living and active, sharper than any two-edged sword, piercing to the division of soul and of spirit, of joints and of marrow, and discerning the thoughts and intentions of the heart. And no creature is hidden from his sight, but all are naked and exposed to the eyes of him to whom we must give account." (Hebrews 4:12–13)

The more God's word is read and the less teaching we do, the more God is working in their hearts. Remember, He is the one doing the teaching.

- Ask the prospect to read the verse out loud.

- Ask open-ended questions. "What do you think this means?" "How would you apply this passage to your life?"

- Acknowledge when the prospect is correct (state, "You are correct.")

If the prospect does not understand the scriptures accurately, then ask them to read the verse again. Perhaps they need a dictionary to define a certain word or read a different translation to get a richer meaning of the text. Do not tell prospects, "you're wrong" or "you're incorrect." Simply ask them to read the scriptures again and acknowledge when they accurately explain the meaning of the text. The Bible says, "All scripture is breathed out by God and profitable for teaching, for reproof, for correction and for training in righteousness, that the man of God may be competent, equipped for every good work." (2 Timothy 3:16).

During a Bible study, we must allow the scriptures to define sin. Let's help the prospect make sin personal, understand the remedy for their sins (salvation), and find the prescription to access the remedy for their sins. The prescription plan that God has given us is the way He wants us to access salvation.

Along the way, listen for the prospect's questions. Questions are great soil indicators of interest. You may try asking open-ended questions, which could cause the prospect to become more comfortable asking their real questions. All questions should be written down, taken seriously, but answered after studying salvation. After all, if you give people deserts and snacks first, most will not be hungry for the main course. The most important questions you must ask everyone are:

- If you were to die now, would you go to heaven?

- Are you willing to do whatever it takes to get to heaven?

- Tell me your conversion story—when you accepted Jesus in your life.

These three questions should begin after the prospects are in full agreement as to what the scriptures say God has done for them (the remedy). You must ask these questions before you study the prescription plan, so that prospects don't project or assume they have already done exactly what the Bible says they should do (even if they haven't).

Finally, some people will respond to the first question "Yes, I am saved." So why would you ask the second question? "Take care, brothers, lest there be in any of you an evil, unbelieving heart, leading you to fall away from the living God." (Hebrews 3:12). The Bible says we can fall away from God, so ask people, "Are you willing to do whatever it takes to get to heaven?" This is the single most important closed-ended question you can ask. By closed-ended, I mean you will only get a yes or no response.

Should the prospect tell you "yes," then you know that they are willing to change their life for God, no matter what it takes. Should the prospect tell you "no," then you must find out immediately what they mean with open-ended questions. Should they tell you that they are only studying with you because they felt bad and are not going to obey, then you may want to postpone the study until they are ready.

Once the prospect acknowledges their understanding and commitment by stating they want to be baptized, we flip the coin and try to talk them out of it. Seriously. Tell them this is a real commitment and you will not baptize them if they are going to just walk right out of the church building never to be seen again. Ask them whether they will promise to study with you weekly. Ask them where they will be next Sunday (perhaps more study on the church will be needed before baptism). Ask them how long they will be faithful.

The process of studying the Bible with people may take months, weeks, or hours. I have been part of all different time frames and have seen some stay faithful and some go astray. We can plant and water, but the rest is between that person and God.

Look at the Mormons. They have a plan, a process, and they execute. They are well-equipped and know what they are going to study and how they are going to study with people. They plan the work and work the plan. Christians, we need to get ourselves equipped, have a plan, and execute it. Know where you are going. Know how you are going to get there. This is simply starting with a plan and executing the plan. Never forget that people are more than just plans, they are not made to be fit into an agenda. So, executing the plan is nothing unless you can take people with you to Jesus and continue to disciple them. You cannot take people with you until you know where they are and what they have questions about.

Open-ended questions during bible study

(Follow along with study guide in the Appendix)

- What would you do if you had a problem, knew you had the problem, and knew there was a solution?

According to 1 John 3:4, the Bible gives the definition of sin, what is it? Who has sinned?

"For all have sinned and fall short of the glory of God," (Romans 3:23).

- Who does the "all" include?

- Have I sinned? What about you?

- What does sin do in our lives immediately?

"but your iniquities have made a separation between you and your God, and your sins have hidden his face from you so that he does not hear" (Isaiah 59:2).

You are correct in thinking that sin causes an immediate separation between God and us.

"For the wages of sin is death, but the free gift of God is eternal life in Christ Jesus our Lord" (Romans 6:23).

- What happens if we continue in that state (in sin)?

These are the open-ended questions I ask during a Bible study. Though they may seem repetitious, the prospect will find a rhythm and predictability that will help guide them through the study. We want them to notice, for example, that in Romans 6:23 we can have eternal life "*in Christ.*" To be "in Christ" is absolutely necessary to eternal life. Actually, the most important information I could share with anyone are those words "in Christ." We cannot be saved outside Christ. Our spiritual blessings right now are found inside Christ and so are our eternal blessings. "Jesus said to him, 'I am the way, and the truth, and the life. No one comes to the Father except through me'" (John 14:6).

We must communicate this during a Bible study. Jesus is absolutely the one we should be committing to. If we are committed to Jesus, we will be committed to His church. The words "in Christ" come up a few times during the study and will certainly come together very logically in Acts 2:38.

Possible questions or comments

In many countries, people ask me during a Bible study, "Are you born again?" "Yes!" I respond. Read the entire conversation Jesus had with Nicodemus in John 3:1–12. "Jesus answered him, 'Truly, truly, I say to you, unless one is born again he cannot see the kingdom of God'" (John 3:3). Jesus first explains the meaning of being born again. It is not a physical birth through the womb of a woman. Second, He explains that rebirth is absolutely necessary to enter into His kingdom. "In Christ" is the most important concept I could teach anyone, and being born again is how to get "in" Christ. The book of Ephesians mentions the words "in Christ" or "with Christ" over thirty times in six chapters.

The Bible says, "By grace you have been saved through faith" (Ephesians 2:8). That is true, but don't forget the context just three verses earlier:

"But God, being rich in mercy, because of the great love with which he loved us, even when we were dead in our trespasses, made us alive together with Christ —by grace you have been saved—and raised us up with him and seated us with him in the heavenly places in Christ Jesus" (Ephesians 2:4-6).

When do we become "in Christ in the heavenly places?" You are correct in thinking, "when we are raised up with Him." When or how are we raised up with Him?

Let us allow the Bible to interpret itself. Paul wrote Ephesians from prison during the same time when he wrote Colossians. Colossians helps us understand Ephesians—they are sister letters. The parallel passage is: "having been buried with him in baptism, in which you were also raised with him through faith in the powerful working of God, who raised him from the dead" (Colossians 2:12). Romans 6:3-5 says the same thing.

How are we raised up with and in Christ?

Through baptism. Read Ephesians 2:5-6 again and you will see that we cannot have the saving grace apart from being raised up in Christ (baptism). They are inseparable. Actually, God's word says that the raising up through faith and baptism is the "powerful working of God." In other words, baptism is a work of God, not man.

The same is true for believing in God. One must believe in God to be saved (Mark 16:16). "Then they said to him,

40

'What must we do, to be doing the works of God?' Jesus answered them, 'This is the work of God, that you believe in him whom he has sent'" (John 6:28–29). Believing is also a work of God. The Bible says "because if you confess with your mouth that Jesus is Lord and believe in your heart that God raised him from the dead, you will be saved. For with the heart one believes and is justified, and with the mouth one confesses and is saved" (Romans 10:9–10). The Bible does not say we have to be baptized in these verses, but it does say this just four chapters prior in the same book (Romans 6:3–5).

What does this verse in Romans 10:9–10 tell us?

You are correct if you said that we are to confess out loud not our sins, but that Jesus is Lord and has been raised from the dead. You are also correct if you said we have to believe that confession with all our heart. Though the passage in Romans said nothing about repenting from sin, we must not forget that God commands us to repent elsewhere in His eternal plan. "And Peter said to them, 'Repent and be baptized every one of you in the name of Jesus Christ for the forgiveness of your sins, and you will receive the gift of the Holy Spirit'" (Acts 2:38).

What are the two commandments here in this verse?

You are correct if you said repent and be baptized.

What if you decide to be baptized and do not repent? What if you repent and decide not to be baptized? Are you fulfilling God's will unto salvation? What did Jesus do about following all of God's will?

"Then Jesus came from Galilee to the Jordan to John, to be baptized by him. John would have prevented him, saying, "I need to be baptized by you, and do you come to me?" But Jesus answered him, "Let it be so now, for thus it is fitting for us to fulfill all righteousness." Then he consented." (Matthew 3:13–15).

Jesus was baptized, and every example we have in the New Testament shows that people were baptized to be saved. What do you think about following all of God's will instead of picking only a few verses here and there to follow? (I have included a picture of a Bible study guide I use toward the back of this book, located in the appendix).

After people obey the gospel, they need to have several follow up Bible studies to ground them in the word of truth. Topics of faith, trials, family, worship, church leadership, evangelism and holy living need to be covered. I would also encourage you to study the book of James with new Christians. The book of James is about living the Christian life.

CHAPTER 4

Sermon design

I've learned from Tom Holland that there are four main sermon types; subject, textual, expository and biographical. Subject sermons are those by which a subject leads us through the main points. Therefore, you could have many different verses from many different books or chapters that contribute to covering the subject.

Why should we use subject sermons? Subject sermons allow us to address specific doctrine. For example, sermons about God's grace, salvation, or worship. Some sermons may be specific to an event like a wedding or a funeral.

Textual sermons usually come from a verse or a passage in the Bible that provides the subject and main points. However, supporting material will be found from different scriptures. Certainly, this sermon type can help you study deeper into the context while using multiple verses from outside the passage to contribute to an in-depth discussion.

Expository sermons are found in one passage alone. That means that the subject, main points and supporting points all come from within that passage. This sermon type allows people to dive into the text to derive its richest meaning, which is why this sermon type is my favorite. (Expository sermons may be a whole chapter or even a whole book in one setting, if you are brief).

Biographical sermons are about people in the Bible. For example, one sermon may be about Hannah or Paul. The subject is the person. The points may come from different verses or one passage. See the chart below with more information:

Areas	Subject sermons	Textual sermons	Expository sermons	Biographical sermons
Sermon subject	Subject could be anything, such as love, grace, or baptism.	The subject comes from one passage or verse.	Subject comes from one passage.	The person is the subject.
Main points	Main points come from multiple passages, in multiple books.	Main points come from one passage or verse. Supporting points come from other verses or passages.	Main points and supporting points come from one passage.	Main points and supporting points may be fron one passage or different passages.
Strengths	Covers a lot of material about a specific subject or an event.	Will derive more meaning from the text. Flexibility between expository and subject type sermons.	Will derive the most meaning from the text. Will remember the meaning of the passage better.	People relate to stories about other people well.
Weaknesses	The possibility of mis-understanding or misusing the context of multiple passages or verses.	May feel limited in with the main points. If you mis-understand the context your sermon will be in error.	Preacher may feel limited. If you mis-understand the context your sermon will be in error.	Limited to that person (the subject).

Delivery types

Delivering sermons is public speaking. There are a few delivery methods that can be utilized for better presentation. Sermon delivery methods are memorization, script or extemporaneous. Memorizing the sermon word for word and presenting it, can be useful but extremely inflexible. Naturally you may be talking over the audience instead of to the audience. The speaker and the audience may notice a disconnect. This method takes the longest time to prepare.

Preaching from a script or notes is a useful delivery method because preachers may get off track or forget something and the notes are an excellent guide. Preaching from notes takes the least amount of preparation because the preacher writes everything he needs to say on the notes. That means they do not have to practice delivering the sermon as much. The weakness is that the preacher may be looking down too often and sound too scripted. Further, the preacher is inclined to read while speaking and thinking at the same time which may cause him to stumble across the words. This also may create a disconnect with the audience. However, when used sparingly, notes can be very helpful. In some cases, reading quotes or facts or statistics are best done by holding the paper up for the audience to see that you are reading from a legitimate source. Inexperienced speakers may use notes excessively, so be careful with this delivery method.

Extemporaneous delivery is a nice blend between memorization and script. Tom Holland encouraged me to use the extemporaneous method of preaching. This method has become my favorite because it gives me flexibility while allowing me to make the greatest connection with the audience. Utilizing this method, one might make a very simple sermon outline (like I have provided) and have that outline memorized. The preacher may have the outline written down on an index card in his Bible. He uses his knowledge to navigate through the sermon while staying on track with the outline in his mind. Textual and expository sermons work very nicely with the extemporaneous delivery method because your outline and points are almost all from the passage of scripture you're preaching from.

The Sermon

Think of your sermon as an airplane ride. When you ride on an airplane, you remember the take-off and you remember the landing. Even if it's a bumpy ride during the flight, you will remember a good take off and a good landing. The take-off is the introduction. The landing is the conclusion and a sermon is not a sermon without application. The preacher must help people apply the scriptures to their life. Scriptures must become real to them. In fact, the preacher's main responsibility in a sermon is to illuminate what is already there or highlight what is written (in the Bible).

The preacher's job is to take life experiences, the word of God—mixed with his personality—to admonish people so they can understand God's word and be motivated to live it. The only way he can successfully do this is to know how to study the Bible, how to develop sermons, and to know the congregation, the individuals, and what they are going through. When the preacher knows the people, he can relate to them and they will relate to him.

The sermon outlines included in this book are laid out in the same outline format. You will notice a title, a scripture text, followed by a purpose statement. The purpose statement is meant for you to say plainly to your audience so they know the purpose of the lesson you are teaching. The purpose statement can also be used as a transition statement between each main point.

Next is your body or main points of the sermon. Usually there are only three or four points with supporting points or material for each main point. The reason there are only three or four points is that people can only remember a few points each time you speak. You want people to remember the main points. Last is a conclusion. Feel free to customize these sermons however you think will be most helpful.

The Hook

At the beginning of each sermon, it's critical to make a connection with the audience. This sets their mind at ease and also sets your mind at ease. The audience will be wondering how well you will do or if you are nervous. Your first impression will set the tone.

Therefore, your introduction is incredibly important. The introduction should connect the speaker with the audience, but should also gain the audience's attention for the sermon. Introductions are like fishing. You use a lure or bait and a hook. A successful introduction hooks your audience. You may sing a song or tell a joke or a story that connects the audience with you and the sermon you intend to deliver. You may use a power pause to get their attention (more on power pauses below).

The Body

The body of the sermon usually has three or four points. The audience is only going to be able to digest three or four points. Your purpose statement may be used as a transitional statement in between each point to emphasize the overall theme of the sermon. If you do not use the purpose statement as a transitional sentence, make a transitional statement that will make sense and help the audience to move from one point to another.

Body Mechanics

While preaching it is important to use good posture. Standing up tall with your chest slightly lifted toward the ceiling is good posture. Good posture allows for good breath support which enables the preacher to preach louder and longer. You must speak to the person furthest away from you so that they can hear you. An older lady told me "Young man, I can't hear most people, they just look nice. But I could hear you well, thank you for a good sermon."

Posture also communicates confidence (the audience needs to know and feel that you are confident about God's word). Eye contact is critical when communicating interpersonally and publicly. Look people in the eyes when speaking, and your message will be taken more personally and be more meaningful to your audience.

Use gestures intentionally. Gestures are body position, hand movements, and facial expressions. Use gestures that will enhance your points and flow well with your sermons. Gestures may be used to get attention or keep the attention of the audience. Be careful of inappropriate gestures or postures such as licking your lips constantly, leaning too far forward over the pulpit, or frowning the entire time. A good communicator utilizes posture and gestures to work with his message. For example, leaning forward and speaking more quietly brings the audience to you and brings you to the audience to make a stronger connection or a strong point.

Powerful Sermons

There are a few things you can do to purposely make your sermon more powerful. Using pauses, rhyming words or words that start with the same sound, or speeding up/slowing down, and speaking loudly or softly. You will also need to speak to the different listener types in the audience.

When communicating a sermon, the speaker must reach everyone. There are three types of listeners to whom you will be preaching.

1. People of detail. They want to know **facts and detailed** information that is challenging. (Context, dates, history, key words defined)
2. People of purpose. They want to know the **purpose** (the purpose statement says it all) but they also want to clearly understand the **application** to their life.
3. People of feeling. They want to know how to **feel** and **react** to the sermon and how it will make them feel or other people feel.

It is important to reach all these listeners. In order to address every listener, you must answer several questions. People of detail want your sermon to answer (in detail) the question "What are we talking about?" In order to address the people of purpose, your sermon needs to state what is being talked about (purpose statement) and answer the questions "Why does this matter?" and "How do I apply this to my life?" To address people of feeling your sermon needs to answer the questions, "How will this make me feel?" or "How will this make others feel?" When you want to address all listeners in one sermon, ensure your sermon answers "What, how, and why?"

To reach all listener types, pauses, rhyming words, volume, and pitch are used to gain and keep the listener's attention. The pause is when you stop speaking. Make sure you finish a complete sentence and make eye contact with your audience. Be still and remain quiet for half a minute. During the first 10 seconds, you'll hear rustling of the people in their seats. After 20 seconds, almost half of the congregation will be making eye contact with you and some beginning to wonder if you forgot what you were saying.

Once you've been quiet for 30 seconds you will have captivated your audience, continue speaking. If I use the pause, it is usually only once during the sermon. It is best to use the pause between major points of the sermon. Sometimes I use the pause in the very beginning when I first stand up to preach. I stand up, and make eye contact with the congregation without saying anything for about 15 seconds. Then I begin to speak. You can gain the attention of your audience with a pause.

Voice fluctuation is a very powerful tool. Speaking softly brings the audience towards you, allowing you to make an important point. Speaking softly is something you do rarely because some people may not hear you. Speaking to the back of the room is loud, which is necessary for people to hear you well and communicates confidence to the audience. Speaking very loud and raising your voice is good when used very purposefully and seldom during the message. Articulating very clearly is incredibly important and often overlooked. Do not use filler words like "uh, umm, and". Many times, people think much faster than the speaker is able to speak. If the speaker can speak quickly and clearly (articulating words) and using gestures the audience will be more captivated as they have less time to think about other things.

Remember that people think much faster than you can speak. Getting rid of filler words (um, ah,) and speaking faster, to the point, will keep the mind of your audience attentive to your message. Using words that rhyme or that start with the same sounds are great tools to help your audience remember your points of your sermon. As preachers, we want our audience to listen, hear, and retain what they heard, and apply what they heard in their life. You can further emphasize points by speeding up and then slowing down. Sometimes I will speak faster and faster, then slow completely down to emphasize a short sentence or word. I might also speak loudly, or softly when emphasizing a short sentence or word.

Repetition will always help our minds remember something. If you use the purpose statement as a transition statement between each major point, including the conclusion, people will hear the purpose statement multiple times in an hour and will probably remember the purpose of your sermon.

For example, in this sermon:

TITLE: What God Can Do Through You
TEXT: Judges 2

PURPOSE STATEMENT:
God can do great things through individuals, despite the people around them.
(Read the purpose statement in full [first time])

INTRODUCTION:

1. The people of Israel were evil (Judges 2:11)
   A. The world was full of evil people during Noah's time.

"But God can do great things through individuals." (Transition Statement)

2. The Lord raised up the judges (Judges 2:16)
   A. God has always had someone that was His faithful follower. God raises up leaders Abraham, Moses, Samuel.

"God can do great things through individuals." (Transition Statement)

3. The Lord saved the people through the judge (Judges 2:18)
   A. The presence of one righteous person influences people and God recognizes that
      i. Think about Abraham and Lot and how Lot was saved from Sodom and Gomorrah.

"God can do great things through individuals, despite the people around them." (Transition Statement)

CONCLUSION:

It doesn't matter what people do around us, before us, or after us. We have the opportunity to save people by the power of the Gospel God has given us.

Think of all the people who were saved under the righteous judge. God can do great things through you.

The above sermon is just an outline and the supporting points need to be developed, they need more information. However, you can see a transition statement in bold between each point which helps people remember the purpose of your sermon.

Chapter 5

Preaching from the Patriarchs

In all honesty, we are borrowing the words of almighty God. So, we really do not own our sermons, God does. I give everyone permission to make copies of these sermons or to use these sermons in any way that will be helpful for preaching, the church, the lost or any edification whatsoever.

You will notice in this chapter and the chapters to follow, that each sermon is designed in an outline format with a title, scripture, purpose statement, introduction, several points, and a conclusion. It is the preacher's job to arrange these sermons in a way that is applicable to the audience and relevant to their lives. The introductions need to be developed with a "hook", to get the audience's attention. Though the purpose statement is provided, there may be times you will repeat the purpose statement (or at least part of it) in-between each point, or you may find the purpose statement is only worth stating once in the beginning. The reason for stating the purpose statement is to help your audience understand where they are going or what they are studying so they can stay with you and retain what they have learned.

The sermons in this book are divided into chapter segments. This chapter starts during the "dispensation" or time period of the patriarchs. This dispensation or specific time lasted from Adam until Moses when God spoke to the fathers of the families directly.

TITLE: Brotherly Love
TEXT: Genesis 13:1-12

PURPOSE STATEMENT:
Unity is more important than possessions or wealth.

INTRODUCTION:

1. Abraham
   - A. He was rich.
   - B. He traveled to a new place.
   - C. He was the leader and God was speaking to him.

2. Lot
   - A. Lot was younger than Abram.
   - B. Lot was his nephew.
   - C. Lot traveled with Abram (Lot followed him).

   These men were like brothers. They were friends and family. **Unity is more important than possessions or wealth.**

3. The problem
   - A. The land could not support both Lot and Abram.
   - B. Their herdsmen were fighting with one another.
     - i. What about our friends? Do our friends cause problems with our family or fellow Christians? How do we respond?

4. The resolution
   - A. Abram offers Lot the first choice.
   - B. Lot chooses the better land.
   - C. The better land or opportunity for Lot was filled with wicked people (See vs. 13.) Sometimes what appeals to the eye is not always better.

i. 1 Corinthians 6:1-8, especially verse 7, "Suffer wrong or be defrauded for your brother's sake."

CONCLUSION:

When we find ourselves at odds with our family or with our Church family, give your brother or sister the first choice. Allow someone else to choose the better end. Be happy with what you have and work with it and you will be blessed.

TITLE: The Godhead
TEXT: Genesis 1:26

PURPOSE STATEMENT:
God is the Father, Son and Holy Spirit

INTRODUCTION:

Who is God?

1. God created everything in the beginning, **because He is God** (Genesis 1:1).
    A. God has always been in existence. God created everything (Genesis 1:1).
    B. God is known as the master mind who plans everything.

2. Jesus, the Son of God, **because He is God** (Genesis 1:26).
    A. Jesus has always existed with God. However, for a brief time he became human to die for our sins. (Notice 1 Corinthians 10:4; John 1:1-4, 14 is referring to Jesus, and Colossians 1:15-17).
    B. Jesus is known as the executor of God's plan. He carries out God's plan. He created creation (Colossians 1:15-17) and died on the cross, fulfilling God's plan.

3. The Holy Spirit was there in the beginning **because He is God** (Genesis 1:2).
    A. The Holy Spirit is God and God is the Holy Spirit.
    B. The Holy Spirit was hovering over the waters (Genesis 1:2).
    C. The Holy Spirit is known as the beautifier, comforter and sustainer of God's plan (John 16:7, 13).

CONCLUSION:

God is eternal and has no beginning and no end. God is the
father, Son and Holy Spirit. We should always respect that.

TITLE: God Made Women
TEXT: Genesis 2:22

PURPOSE STATEMENT:
What purpose do women have?

INTRODUCTION:

Women are very important. They are our wives, mothers, daughters and sisters.

1. God made women to follow Him.
    A.   God created everything, including Adam and Eve. God expected Eve to follow him, but she ate of tree God told her not to. Adam and Eve were both made "in the image of God" (Genesis 1:26).

2. Women are for companionship.
    A.   God saw that Adam was lonely (Genesis 2:18). Woman was the only suitable companion for man. Therefore, when a woman is married, she is to be held fast to her husband (to be with him).

3. Women were created to help man (Genesis 2:18).
    A.   The marriage relationship is beautiful when the woman wants to help her husband be successful in life.

4. Women were created to bear children.
    A.   Be fruitful and multiply (Genesis 1:28).
    B.   1 Timothy 2:15

CONCLUSION:

Marriage is beautiful. A husband and wife who are working together following God is truly respected and admired by all who see such a great relationship

TITLE: God Made Man
TEXT: Genesis 1:26

PURPOSE STATEMENT:
Men have a purpose!

INTRODUCTION:

Men are our husbands, fathers, brothers and sons. They are very important to us.

1. Made in the image of God (Genesis 1:26)
    - A. Men are made in the image of God that is why we respect men.
    - B. Men are made to lead the families. (Colossians 3:18-21)
    - C. Ephesians 5:22-23

2. Made to Work (Genesis 2:15)
    - A. Man was to work in the garden before there was a curse.

3. Made for his wife (2:24)
    - A. Leave his parents, support her. To be fruitful and multiply.
    - B. Husbands love your wife. Love mentioned 3 times (Ephesians 5:25-33).

CONCLUSION:

Man has always had responsibilities even before Adam sinned and cursed him.

TITLE: The Life of Joseph
TEXT: Genesis 37-39

PURPOSE STATEMENT:
We will experience good things and bad things because this is life.

INTRODUCTION:

Our life will have struggles. If you live long enough, you will have pain. You will also have to make sacrifices.

1. His Father favored him (Joseph) (Genesis 37:3).
    A.   Sometimes we have blessings and we feel like God is hearing us.

This is life.

2. His brothers hated him (Genesis 37:5).
    A.   Some people will be jealous of you when you get something.

This is life.

3. He was a servant in Egypt (Genesis 39:1).
    A.   He became the best servant he could be.
    B.   The Lord was with him (Genesis 39:2).
    C.   He was set up by his master's wife and thrown into prison.
    D.   The Lord was with him and Joseph remained steadfast and became the overseer of all the prisoners.

This is life.

4. He ruled Egypt (Genesis 41:39-40).
    A.   Joseph interpreted the dream for Pharaoh.
    B.   Joseph became second highest in command over Egypt and saved his family.

CONCLUSION:

Sometimes we suffer in life. Sometimes we are blessed in life. God always loves us. Let us remain steadfast to the Lord like Joseph and we can go to heaven when we die.

Chapter 6

Sermons from Sinai

Preaching from Sinai represents the Mosaic dispensation. This dispensation marks the end of the patriarchal dispensation. The Mosaic dispensation stared with Moses and ended with Jesus Christ. During this dispensation, God saves His people, the Israelites, from Egypt. The Law, which includes the 10 commandments and worship, sacrifices and priesthood were given during this dispensation. "And Moses summoned all Israel and said to them, 'Hear, O Israel, the statues and the rules that I speak in your hearing today, and you shall learn them and be careful to do them. The LORD our God made a covenant with us in Horeb. Not with our fathers did the Lord make this covenant, but with us, who are all of us here alive today'" (Deuteronomy 5:1-3). Notice the Law (singular) was given from Mount Sinai (or Horeb). The Law was not given to Adam, Abraham, Isaac or Jacob. The scriptures say the Law was given to Moses and the Israelites who came out of Egypt. During this time period, I have selected a few sermons that may be helpful to you and the congregation where you worship.

TITLE: God Hears Us
TEXT: Exodus 2:23-25

PURPOSE STATEMENT:
God hears us and will intervene to guide us and show us the right way.

INTRODUCTION:

God will hear His people.

1. Israel groaned to God.
    A.   Do we have issues, concerns or needs? Do we groan to God?
    B.   Romans 8:23 "we ourselves, who have the first fruits of the Spirit groan inwardly as we wait eagerly for adoption."

God will hear us

2. God heard (them).
    A.   John 9:31 "God does not listen to sinners, but if anyone is a worshiper of God and does His will, God listens to him."

God will intervene in our lives

3. God saw them.
    A.   Psalms 33:13-14
    B.   Luke 18:1-8
        i.   The widow continued asking and changed the Judge's mind.
        ii.   God is our judge who will do the same for us.

CONCLUSION:

In Exodus chapter 3 the Bible says, "The Lord said, 'I have surely seen the affliction of my people who are in Egypt and have heard their cry because of their taskmasters. I know their sufferings, and I have come down to deliver them out of the hand of the Egyptians and to bring them up out of that land to a good and broad land, a land flowing with milk and honey...'" (Exodus 3:7-9).

God will hear us when we groan together and plead for help. God sent Moses to help the people. God will help us today, as He has sent His son. God leads us out of sin, and slavery to sin, to be on a journey with Jesus.

TITLE: Outreach Through Holiness and Agape Love.
TEXT: Leviticus 19

PURPOSE STATEMENT:
Encourage people to love each other, be holy and reach out to their neighbor.

INTRODUCTION:

1. Holiness
   A. Holiness means "Set apart, dedication to/for God."
   B. Our actions are to show we are dedicated to God.
   C. We are a royal priesthood of God now (1 Peter 2:9), so we also have a holiness code. We must offer sacrifices (the fruit of our lips, do good, and share what you have (Hebrews 13:15-16)). Holy living is living by God's standard and by His commandments.

2. Agape
   b. Agape love is the active form of love toward God, fellow man and even enemies by bestowing goodness and kindness to them and expecting nothing in return.
      i. Romans 5:8, which uses the word agape, shows what God did (sent His son as a sacrifice for us, without expecting that we give anything back).
   B. In Leviticus, the Hebrew word is "Ahab", which means, "love like a friend". Ahab has a different meaning than agape love.
   C. So, let us love people even more than Agape, let us love people even like a friend.
   D. Sometimes we may give people kindness by visiting them or praying for them. Sometimes we may give people kindness by studying the

Bible with them or helping them with a work. Helping people doesn't always mean giving people money or giving people gifts.

3. Outreach
    A.   Outreach means to contact other people with the Gospel, the good news of Jesus!
    B.   We will be more effective at reaching the lost for Christ when we are living a Holy life with Agape love.

CONCLUSION:

In this passage, we are not responsible for keeping the Sabbath, nor do we make peace offerings any more. Jesus is the final offering and the Lord's Day, Sunday, is the day we worship God. However, we must still be a Holy people, living a life of Holiness with love.

TITLE: What God Can Do Through You
TEXT: Judges 2 (entire chapter)

PURPOSE STATEMENT:
God can do great things through individuals, despite the people around them.

INTRODUCTION:

You are unique to God. He can do great things through you.

1. The people of Israel were evil (Judges 2:11).
     A. The world was full of evil people during Noah's time.

"But God can do great things through individuals." (Transition Statement)

2. The Lord raised up the judges (Judges 2:16).
     A. God has always had someone that was His faithful follower. God raises up leaders like Abraham, Moses, and Samuel.

 "God can do great things through individuals." (Transition Statement)

3. The Lord saved the people through the judge (Judges 2:18).
     A. The presence of one righteous person influences people and God recognizes that.
     B. Think about Abraham and Lot and how Lot was saved from Sodom and Gomorrah because Abraham was righteous.

"God can do great things through individuals, despite the people around them."

CONCLUSION:

It doesn't matter what people do around us, before us, or after us. We have the opportunity to save people by the power of the Gospel God has given us.

Think of all the people who were saved under the righteous judge. God can do great things through you if you live a righteous life

TITLE: But Moses Said
TEXT: Exodus Chapters 3-4

PURPOSE STATEMENT:
God wants you to tell people about Jesus.

INTRODUCTION:

Moses was a man who ran away from his problems, but God still calls him at the burning bush. God gave him instructions to tell people about him.

1. Who am I? (Exodus 3:11)
    A.   "But", Moses said...I am not good enough.
    B.   Sometimes we think we are not good enough to teach someone the Gospel.
    C.   Moses made excuses, but God provided answers.
    D.   God provides us answers through His word.

    God wants you to tell people about Jesus!

2. They won't believe me. (Exodus 4:1)
    A.   "But" they won't believe me.
    B.   We have doubts, but God doesn't.
    C.   God knew Pharaoh wouldn't let the people go, but still wanted Moses to try.
    D.   God knows some people will listen and some people won't.

    God wants you to tell people about Jesus!

3. I can't speak well. (Exodus 4 :10)
    A.   Moses is almost out of excuses.
    B.   Sometimes we are too hard on ourselves.
    C.   There is usually someone (brother or sister) who can help us, like Aaron.

God wants you to tell people about Jesus!

4. Please send someone else. (Exodus 4:13)
    A. When we have no more excuses, we want someone else to do it.
    B. It's someone else's job to preach.
    C. Our preacher should be the one to go talk to other people, right?
    D. No, we all have responsibility to talk about Jesus Christ.

CONCLUSION:

God is telling you to tell others about him (Mathew 28:19-20). No excuses, it's time to go out and tell people about Jesus. Imagine a church who has members who are loving and kind and always inviting people to their church. Imagine a church who has members that talk about Jesus using the scriptures. The community will be influenced and even changed to be more like Jesus.

Chapter 7

Preaching from the Prophets and Wisdom Literature

TITLE: Be A Man
TEXT: 1 Kings 2:1-3

PURPOSE STATEMENT:
To challenge men to be "a man".

INTRODUCTION:

King David was about to die, and called for his son Solomon. He wanted him to know something really important. He challenged him to be a man. What is a man? What does our culture tell us a man is? What does a man do? The Bible has a definition in 1 Kings 2:1-3.

1. Be strong
    A. Being strong doesn't mean physically, but spiritually strong and mentally strong.
    B. Men bring security to the family.
    C. Men bring stability to the family.
    D. Children look up to their fathers like they will look up to God. God provides, men (fathers) should provide.

2. Be a man
    A. What does your country say a man is? What does the Bible say a man is?
    B. Some think being a man means to get drunk or to be promiscuous with women.
    C. The Bible clearly has an image of what a man should look like and act like. Don't let culture tell you something different than your creator.

D. A man follows God and lives a holy life.

3. Keep the charge of the Lord
    A. A man will keep the charge of the Lord.
    B. David wanted Solomon to know that a real man keeps God's law and follows God's ways. Solomon didn't always do that, but when Solomon wrote Ecclesiastes he ended the book "Fear God and keep his commandments, for this is the whole duty of man" (Ecclesiastes 12:13). Solomon surely remembered his father (King David) telling him this, just before David died.

4. You will prosper.
    A. When a man is strong and keeps God's word, not letting anyone or anything distract him, he will prosper in what he does.
    B. God gives promises and fulfills promises to His faithful followers.

CONCLUSION:

When we do things God's way, we prosper. So, be a man, a man made in the image of God and following after God.

TITLE: Our Shelter in A Time of Storm
TEXT: Isaiah 25:4–5

PURPOSE STATEMENT:
He is our shelter in a time of storm.

INTRODUCTION:

Physically we require air (to breathe) and then look for water, food and security. Where do you look for security?

1. A stronghold to the needy
   A. We don't have to be afraid of poverty, or being hungry. God knows us and sees us. God will be victorious!
   B. To live is Christ and to die is gain (heaven) (Philippians 1:21).

2. A shelter
   A. A shelter from the storm, though it beats against the wall (vs4)
   B. We don't have to worry about problems from the ruthless (people who are against us). God will be like a shelter in the time of storm. Storms may be loud and strong, but the shelter will protect us.
   C. The Church, the people of Christ, is a great shelter (comfort from the troubles of life).

3. A shade
   A. A shade from the heat, like a cloud God puts the heat away.
   B. People can be ruthless, like the heat of the day. But even the heat during the day only lasts a few hours. God will be our shade during the hard times with people and they will leave us alone.

CONCLUSION:

In our hymn books, we have this song "A Shelter in Time of Storm." We can hide in Jesus, he is our defense, and He protects us from storms or "life". God is our shelter. When we trust in God to guide us and protect us He will. Let's find joy and peace in reading the scriptures and praying.

TITLE: The Foundation
TEXT: Isaiah 28:16

PURPOSE STATEMENT:
Jesus is the foundation!

INTRODUCTION:

Foundations are the stronghold and security of buildings and people. Think of buildings, houses, and churches. Think about schools. All of these places have something they are built on. Some are built on rock, or cement, or the dirt. What is your life built on?

1. The location of the foundation.
    A. Zion is the location (Jerusalem Isaiah 2:3).
    B. Builders rejected it (Psalms 118:22).
    C. The Pharisees rejected Him (Matthew 21:42-46).
    D. Acts 4:11

    But Jesus is the foundation!

2. The certainty of the foundation.
    A. Tested stone. Jesus is sure, His foundation is sure.
        i. We can be sure what He tells us is true.
    B. Living stone 1 Peter 2:4
        i.   Spiritual house = the Church
        ii. Holy Priesthood = righteous living
        iii. Acceptable Sacrifice = proper worship

    But Jesus is the foundation!

3. The value of the foundation.
    A. Precious (why?)
        i. Because Jesus was sacrificed for us. A human life given.

75

A. The cornerstone brings all people together. (Eph. 2:11-22)
    i.   Jews/Gentiles
    ii. Members of the (singular) house hold of God.
    iii. Holy

But Jesus is the foundation!

4. The promise of the foundation.
    A. Whoever believes will not be in haste (or put to shame).
    B. Gentiles can be saved (Romans 9:30-33).
    C. Romans 9:24 "The Gentiles".

CONCLUSION:

Jesus is the foundation. God can save anyone (Romans 10:13).
Let's be careful that we are on the foundation. Let's be careful how we build on the foundation (1 Corinthians 3:10-13).

TITLE: Stubborn Children
TEXT: Isaiah 30:1-2

PURPOSE STATEMENT:
God's ways are better than our ways.

INTRODUCTION:

Have you known anyone who is stubborn? Have you seen any children who are stubborn? Have your children ever been stubborn?

1. Our plans
   A. The Bible calls people "Stubborn" when they carry out plans that are not God's plans.
   B. Sometimes we don't wait on the Lord, instead, we depend on ourselves, money or people.
   C. Who should we depend on?

   God's ways are better

2. Our friends
   A. God's anger is kindled when we choose not to make an alliance with His Spirit.
   B. The Bible says people will make the wrong alliances or friends and sin even more.

   God's ways are better

3. Our direction
   A. Do we ask God for the directions?
   B. The Bible says the Israelites went away without direction.
   C. Can you know where you are going without direction?

D. God's word gives us direction, shelter and hope.
E. Are we lost? Are we looking to other people for direction, shelter and hope?
F. The Israelites even looked to Pharaoh and Egypt for shelter and hope (which corrupted them spiritually.)

CONCLUSION:

Children listen to your parents. Parents listen to your God. **God's ways are better.**

TITLE: The Way
TEXT: Isaiah 35:8

PURPOSE STATEMENT:
God's way is the higher way.

INTRODUCTION:

"There is a way that seems right to a man, but its end is the way to death" (Proverbs 14:12 and 16:25).

1. What is it? (Isaiah 35:8)
    A. The Highway is a higher way of life.
    B. The <u>W</u>ay, notice the capital W.
        i.   Acts 9:2, 19:9, 23 and 24:14, 22
        ii. Proverbs 15:9 there is a way of the wicked.
    C. The Way is Holy.
        i.   Jesus said "I am the way, the truth, and the life" (John 14:1-6).

2. Who is it? (Isaiah 35:8-9)
    A. The Way belongs to those who walk on it. The people are the church (Colossians 1:18).
    B. No lion (Satan), nor beast should be there (1 Peter 5:8).
    C. The redeemed shall walk there. It is a way of righteousness.
        i.   The narrow way (Matthew 7:13-14).

3. Where is it? (35:10)
    A. Zion (referring to heaven).
    B. The ransomed of the Lord shall return (heaven). Return to their creator.
    C. Everlasting joy (heaven).
    D. Sorrow and sighing shall flee away.

79

CONCLUSION:

Are you **in** the Way? Are you **on** the way (to heaven)?

TITLE: God's Comfort
TEXT: Isaiah 40:1-2

PURPOSE STATEMENT:
God brings us comfort.

INTRODUCTION:

The book of Isaiah is called the small Bible because the book of Isaiah looks like the Bible. The Bible has 66 books and Isaiah has 66 chapters. The first 39 books of the Bible are about Judgment, history, and wisdom (the Old Testament). The first 39 chapters of Isaiah are about judgment, history and wisdom (there are some exceptions). The last 27 chapters of Isaiah are about salvation, comfort and hope. The last 27 books of the Bible (New Testament) are about salvation, comfort and hope.

1. Warfare has ended.
   A.   Israel's war, physical war was ended. They were seeking comfort.
   B.   We are in a spiritual war for God against the Devil and evil. (Ephesians 6:10-20)
   C.   A soldier is enrolled in the Army (Christians are enrolled for God to carry out His will) (2 Timothy 2:4).
   D.   Paul said, "Fight the good fight" and he said of himself, "I have Fought the good fight, finished the race" (1Timothy 6:12; 2 Timothy 4:7).
   E.   We will finish fighting for Jesus when we die.

2. Iniquity is pardoned.
   A.   Israel's sins are forgiven
   B.   When we obey God, are sins are forgiven for sure.
   C.   Once we have been raised with Christ, we have God's grace for us specifically (Ephesians 2:5-6; Colossians 2:12).

     D. Being raised means being baptized. After baptism God's grace will continue to save us when we sin and ask for forgiveness.

3. Received double (Pardon for sins)
     A. Israel was not only forgiven, but released from captivity.
     B. Sins forgiven= Mercy
     C. Sins forgiven and given freedom in Christ to go to heaven= Grace
     D. Mercy is holding back judgment. Grace is holding back judgment and giving something we don't deserve.
     E. What are you held captive by? What makes your heart race, what are you so excited about that it takes first place in your heart? Are you held captive by sin?
     F. Jesus said "The truth will set you free" (John 8:32).
     G. A bondservant is a free man in the Lord (1 Corinthians 7:22-24) we can be free because of Christ, but a bondservant to Christ.
     H. "For Freedom, Christ has set us free, stand firm therefore and do not submit again to a yoke of slavery" (Galatians 5:1).
     I. We are released from sin and given the opportunity of heaven as Christians. Let us be confident in that.

CONCLUSION:

When conflict arises, priorities are made. Let's encourage people as they near death that their warfare has ended, their sins are forgiven and they will receive a pardon.

Title: Have You Not Heard?
Text: Isaiah 40:28-31

PURPOSE STATEMENT:
The Lord is the everlasting God.

INTRODUCTION:

The eternal nature of God is hard to understand because our minds are limited by time and space. God is not limited by time or space. What do we do when we come across difficult concepts about God that are hard to understand? We walk by faith, not by sight.

The Lord is the everlasting God.

1. The Lord is everlasting.
    A. Jesus is the creator of the earth.
    B. The Bible says Jesus is the Alpha and Omega, the beginning and the end (Revelation 1:8).
    C. Colossians 1:18, John 1:1-4. God planned everything, Jesus created everything. The Holy Spirit sustains everything.

The Lord is the everlasting God.

2. He does not grow faint.
    A. He (Jesus) does not grow weary.
    B. His understanding is unsearchable.
    C. He has the power to give power to the faint.
    D. Youths shall faint, but the Lord is everlasting.

The Lord is the everlasting God.

3. Those who wait for the Lord
    A. Shall be renewed.
    B. Shall have wings of an eagle.

C.   Shall run and not be weary; they shall walk and not faint.
D.   Because the Lord is the everlasting God.

When you understand this passage, you will read it with the right inflections (Read vs 31 again).

Because the Lord is the everlasting God.

CONCLUSION:

The Lord is everlasting and He is God. Be blessed and encouraged that He has unlimited energy and strength and loves you in such a way to give you energy and renew your strength.

Title: The Description of Jesus.
Text: Isaiah 9:6

PURPOSE STATEMENT:
Surely, this is Jesus.

INTRODUCTION:

This is a prophecy about Jesus Christ.

1. Wonderful counselor
   A. John 4, He was counseling the woman at the well.
   B. Jesus went to "console" the people because of Lazarus. (John 11:19)

   Surely, this is Jesus

2. Mighty God
   A. Col. 1:15-16
   B. John 1:1-4

   Surely, this is Jesus

3. Everlasting Father
   A. Jesus is God.
   B. Phil. 2:5-11
   C. Hebrews 13:8

   Surely, this is Jesus

4. Prince of peace
   A. Luke 24:36 (context)
   B. John 20:21
   C. Acts 10:36
   D. Matt. 5:9

   Surely, this is Jesus

CONCLUSION:

Jesus is all things because He is God.

Title: The Lord's salvation
Text: Isaiah 12

PURPOSE STATEMENT:
Let's find joy in salvation!

INTRODUCTION:

Only 3 chapters in Isaiah have six verses (4, 12, and 20) and chapter 12 is full of thanksgiving. In such a short transcription, the word "praise" appears once, "thanks" and "joy" each appear twice, salvation appears three times, and "Lord" appears four times.

1. Salvation (1-2)
    A. "Your anger turned away that you might comfort me."
    B. This is grace. Mercy is turning away anger. Grace is turning away anger and comforting.
    C. You are my SALVATION!
    D. I will trust in you. This trust is "sure" and "bold" and "confident"
    E. Now faith is the assurance of things hoped for, the conviction of things not seen" (Hebrews 11:1).
    F. GOD WILL SAVE YOU AND BE YOUR STRENGTH AND YOUR SONG.

    Let's find joy in salvation

2. Joy and thanks (3-4)
    A. Because we are saved let us rejoice and give thanks.
    B. We will draw from salvation, **JOY.**

    Let's find joy in salvation

3. Proclaim and sing (4-6)

87

A. When we have a great salvation and when we are so joyful, we will SING praises to the Lord.
B. Have you heard people singing praises while they are working, cooking, cleaning, and walking down the road? We should be singing with joy because God is saving us!
C. God saved us (past tense). God is saving us (present tense) as we follow Him!
D. We sing about this salvation, but we also proclaim it!
E. Our proclamation should be to our neighbor. Our proclamation should be to the **world!**

CONCLUSION:

This is a short chapter in Isaiah 12, but a powerful reminder that we must be joyful about being saved every day.

Title: Offerings to God
Text: Isaiah 1:11–20

PURPOSE STATEMENT:
It matters to God what we offer him.

INTRODUCTION:

"I have had enough of burnt offerings of rams and the fat of well-fed beasts; I do not delight in the blood of bulls or lambs, or of goats" (Isaiah 1:11).
"For it is impossible for the blood of bulls and goats to take away sins" (Hebrews 10:4).

1. Our problem (Isaiah 1:13)
    A. Bring no more vain worship (vain offerings).
    B. What is vain worship?
    C. Sin, active sin by the worshiper.
    D. When you make prayers, God will not listen (vs.15).
    E. Vain worship is wrong worship. We sing only (Ephesians 5:19-20 and Colossians 3:16-17). Men lead the worship (1 Timothy 2:8; 1 Corinthians 14:33-34).
    F. Vain worship is a burden to God, it makes Him weary.

    It matters to God what we offer him

2. Our response (Isaiah 1:16)
    A. Make yourselves clean/save yourself from this crooked generation (Acts 2:40).
    B. Work out your own salvation (Philippians 2:12).
    C. Wash=baptism. Washing of regeneration (Titus 3:5).
    D. Remove evil deeds, cease evil. Learn to do good, justice, correct oppression (Isaiah 1:16-17).

It matters to God what we offer him.

3. The Lord's promise (Isaiah 1:18)
   - A. Let us reason together
   - B. Sins = Scarlet
   - C. Forgiveness = White as snow
   - D. Willingness/obedience = eat the good (reward/blessings).
   - E. If you refuse/you will be eaten (opposite of eating/reward).

It matters to God what we offer him.

CONCLUSION:

Worship/righteous living matters. "Therefore, let us be grateful for receiving a kingdom that cannot be shaken, and thus let us offer to God acceptable worship, with reverence and awe, for our God is a consuming fire" (Hebrews 12:28).

Title: Prophecy About the Church
Text: Isaiah 2:2-5

PURPOSE STATEMENT:
God promised the church would be exactly like this.

INTRODUCTION:

This is a prophecy about the Church.

1. When- "It shall come in the latter days" (Isaiah 2:2)
   - A. Last days (Hebrews 1:2)
   - B. The SDA church started in American in 1800's.
   - C. The Church of Christ started with Jesus and the Holy Spirit of God in year 33 at Pentecost in the "last days."

2. What- "the mountain of the house of the Lord shall be established as the highest of the mountains," (Isaiah 2:2)
   - A. The house of the Lord will be **Established**.
   - B. The temple was already built; therefore, this was a new house to be established.
   - C. Jesus said He built it (Matthew 16:18, Hebrews 3:5).
   - D. The house is the body of Christ (Ephesians 2:19 and 1 Peter 2:5).
   - E. Now Jesus is over God's House. We (Christians) are the house (Hebrews 3:6).

3. Who- "and all the nations shall flow to it and many peoples shall come and say:" (Isaiah 2:3)
   - A. All nations present (represented by Jews only Acts 2:5-7).
   - B. Also, Acts 10 = Gentiles (all nations) were accepted.
   - C. Acts 2:39 says, "for all".
   - D. May peoples 3,000 people were baptized (Acts 2:41).

E.   More people were baptized and their number was 5,000 (Acts 4:5).

4. Where- "for out of Zion shall go the law, and the word of the Lord from Jerusalem" (Isaiah 2:3)
    A.   Mt. Zion = Jerusalem
    B.   This is the location where the established house or "church" of God would begin.
    C.   Jerusalem is the location where the church began. If a church did not start in Jerusalem, it's not the real church.
    D.   Acts 2 is the fulfillment of this prophecy and Acts 2:5 "dwelling in Jerusalem".
    E.   The SDA church follows the 10-commandment law given to Moses on Mount Sinai.
    F.   The Church of Christ was started by Jesus on Mount Zion in Jerusalem.
    G.   These are two different mountains.

5. Why- "For out of Zion shall go the law and the word of the LORD from Jerusalem" (Isaiah 2:3-4)
    A.   Teach us His ways.
    B.   Walk in His path.
    C.   Peace in the church.
    D.   The church and peace will exist for all nations.

CONCLUSION:

God promised His church. He told us what, when, who, where and why. Finally, the Bible says that we the Church of Christ, should not practice war anymore. We should not fight with our neighbor and force them to be a Christian because Jesus will judge all people (Isaiah 2:4). What about you? Are you going to be in the Church? Are you going to walk in the light of the Lord? (Isaiah 2:5)

TITLE: Stumbled and Fallen
TEXT: Isaiah 3:8–11

PURPOSE STATEMENT:
What goes around comes around.

INTRODUCTION:

You have heard of the saying what goes around comes around.
The Bible tells us how this phenomenon works in progression.

1. Against God.
   - A.   Our speech can make us stumble before God.
   - B.   Be slow to speak (James 1:19).
   - C.   Our tongue is evil and stains us (James 3:5-6).

2. They proclaim their sin.
   - A.   The progression of sin (Psalms 1:1).
   - B.   Walk around sin, stand in sin, and sit in sin.
   - C.   When you sit in sin, you are comfortable sinning.
   - D.   When you are comfortable in sin, you ask others to join you (Romans 1:32).

3. They have brought evil on themselves.
   - A.   What his hands have dealt out shall be to him (vs.11).
   - B.   God says "Vengeance is mine, I will repay, says the Lord" (Romans 12:19).
   - C.   What goes around comes around.

CONCLUSION:

Finally, the Bible says, "Tell the righteous that it shall be well with them, for they shall eat the fruit of their deeds." When you do good, good will come back around. Let's help people who have stumbled and have fallen, because what goes around comes around.

TITLE: The Mediator
TEXT: 1 Samuel 2:25

PURPOSE STATEMENT:
Christians have the greatest mediator (Hebrews 9:15).

1. What is a mediator?
    - A. Someone who stands between two parties (or people) to work through their differences.
    - B. In this case God and man are the parties.

2. Who is the mediator?
    - A. Moses was, the priests where.
    - B. Now there is one mediator Jesus (1 Tim. 2:5; Hebrews 12:24).
    - C. Jesus is also the one priest (Hebrews 4:14-15).

3. Why do we need a mediator?
    - A. God is Holy. God does not fellowship sin.
    - B. God wants to fellowship with us.
    - C. If we sin, we have an advocate (Jesus) who will intercede for us (1 John 2:1-3).

CONCLUSION:

Jesus is the greatest mediator giving you the greatest opportunity to fellowship with God.

TITLE: The Law
TEXT: Nehemiah 9:13-14

PURPOSE STATEMENT:
Where did God give the law?

INTRODUCTION:

The Law was given and then a NEW Law was given.

1. God came down on Mt. **Sinai** (where).
    A.   The law was given in Horeb. Mount Sinai is in Horeb (Deuteronomy 5:1-3).

2. God gave them rules, laws, statutes, commandments (what).
    A.   The Ten Commandments (Deuteronomy 5:6-21).

3. Made known to them (when).
    A.   That day, the Sabbath (Nehemiah 9:13-14 and Deuteronomy 5:3). Not with people before (Adam, Noah, Abraham, Isaac and Jacob). This law was for the Israelites. This law was not for the gentiles and is not for us today.
    B.   A law, by Moses
    C.   Deuteronomy 5:1-3

4. The NEW Law.
    A.   The New Law coming, NOT like the first covenant (Jeremiah 31:31-32).
    B.   Hebrews 8:13

CONCLUSION:

The law was given to certain people, for a certain time, from a certain mountain.

TITLE: The Priests, The People and The Promise
TEXT: Malachi (The whole book)

PURPOSE STATEMENT:
Follow God because Jesus is coming!

INTRODUCTION:

There was a time of silence from God. Not a word was spoken, or written, nor was there a prophet with a message or a sign from the heavens. For nearly 500 years God's people were waiting...until John the Immerser was baptizing people for repentance in the river Jordan. God left the people with a message prior to the 500 years of silence He left them with a book. The last book of the Old Testament, just before the New Testament, is Malachi.

1. The Priests (Malachi 1:6-2:9)
    A. Honor- Are we honoring God with our worship (Malachi 1:6-7)?
    B. Polluted worship. Are we giving God the right worship? (Malachi 1:7-8, 13).
    C. Polluted priests. Covenant with Levi (Mal. 2:4-7). The priests turned aside, caused many to stumble. Be careful of preachers who are not following the Bible accurately.

2. The People (Malachi 2:10-17, 3:8-18)
    A. "Faithless to one another". God expects us to help strengthen each other. (Galatians 6:2).
    B. The result of their faithlessness = unanswered prayers
    C. Unfaithful to their wives. (See 1 Peter 3:7) God is seeking Godly offspring.
    D. Wearied God- Even the People began saying evil is good in the sight of the Lord.
    E. Robbed God- Will a man rob God? Yet you are robbing me, the whole nation of you" (Malachi 3:9-10). Bring the full tithe.

3. The Promise (Malachi 3:1-7, 4:1-6)
  A.　The messenger "Behold, I send my messenger and he will prepare the way before me" (Malachi 3:1).
    i.　Elijah to come (Malachi 4:5). John the Immerser (Luke 7:24-28). Though John wasn't Elijah himself, he was like Elijah (Luke 1:17; Matthew 11:13).
    ii.　The Lord "And the Lord whom you seek will suddenly come to his temple and the messenger of the covenant in whom you delight, behold, he is coming says the Lord of hosts" (Malachi 3:1). This is Jesus (Luke 2:27; John 2:14; Matthew 21:12; Mark 12:35; Luke 20:1).
  B.　Jesus did come, but they missed it! Some people got it, they prepared and obeyed, but a lot of people missed Jesus Christ!

CONCLUSION:

We are living in the promise right now. Yet Jesus issued another promise. He is coming back only one more time. Don't miss it! Don't miss it like they've missed it. Live in the promise.

Wisdom (Psalms, Proverbs, Ecclesiastes, Job)

TITLE: The Progression of Sin
TEXT: Psalms 1:1-6

PURPOSE STATEMENT:
The sin of man has a course.

INTRODUCTION:

How do we trap animals? How do we get trapped by Satan? Sin is a trap!

1. Walks around sin.
    - A.   People will begin walking around sin, curious, but not doing anything wrong yet.
    - B.   Their hearts have begun to be darkened (Romans 1:21).

2. Stands in sin.
    - A.   When people become comfortable walking around sin, they stand in it, joining hands.
    - B.   God will give them up (Romans 1:24).

3. Sits down in sin.
    - A.   Once people are now sinning, they sit down to establish themselves and even others in sin.
        - i.   Romans 1:32

CONCLUSION:

Blessed is the man who does not do these things. (Read Psalms 1:2-6).
We will be like a tree by the water, strong and full of life if we follow the Lords word and way.

Title: God's Lot for Man
TEXT: Ecclesiastes 2:10

PURPOSE STATEMENT:
God wants us to enjoy our work.

INTRODUCTION:

In Genesis chapter 2:15, before the fall of man, God expected man to work.

1. Find enjoyment in his toil (Ecclesiastes 2:24).
    A. Are we trying to find what makes us happy or are we going to be happy with whatever we find?

2. Rejoice in work (Ecclesiastes 3:22).
    A. In order to be happy in life, we must learn to rejoice where we are right now. Even if we don't' have a job now, we should rejoice and find a reason to have joy.

3. Our reward is our toil (Ecclesiastes 2:10).
    A. When we have work to do, that is a gift from God and we should rejoice about that.

CONCLUSION:

Nothing replaces hard work. Let's enjoy the simple things, that's what God had in mind for us.

TITLE: Jesus, The Son, The King
TEXT: Psalms 2:1-12

PURPOSE STATEMENT:
The first prophecy of Jesus in Psalms.

Introduction:

The Bible uses different terms to describe who Jesus is to us.

1. The Anointed. Kings take council against the LORD and <u>His</u>
   Anointed.
        A.   Notice the capital "A" in Anointed. (Indicating Jesus)

2. <u>The **King**</u> on **Zion.**
        A.   Notice the capital "K" in King (indicating Jesus).
        B.   Notice the capital "Z" in Zion (indicating the place.) The place of Zion is either heaven or Jerusalem.

3. The **Son.**
        A.   Notice the capital "S" in Son.
        B.   Acts 13:26-35

CONCLUSION:

Jesus is the Anointed. He is the King and He is the Son of God.

TITLE: Job Saw the Resurrection
TEXT: Job: 19:25-27

PURPOSE STATEMENT:
Job saw that the resurrection would happen.

INTRODUCTION:

The purpose statement of Job is found in Job 28:28.

1. I <u>know</u> my Redeemer lives.
      A.   Knowing is faith. Faith is knowing without seeing.
      B.   Hope is an expectation based on knowing (faith).

2. <u>He</u> will stand.
      A.   Jesus is faithful. He cannot deny himself.

3. My skin destroyed, I will see God.
      A.   Hope= I will see God. An expectation based on faith.

CONCLUSION:

We will be resurrected one day. Will you be ready?

TITLE: Seeking Wisdom
TEXT: Proverbs 2:1-6

PURPOSE STATEMENT:
God gives us wisdom.

INTRODUCTION:

The world can never match up to the wisdom God has given us through His word.

1. If you receive
   - A. Acts 2:41 "so those who <u>received</u> his word were baptized..."
   - B. "Let the wise hear and increase in learning" (Proverbs 1:5).
   - C. "The fear of the Lord is the beginning of knowledge; fools despise wisdom and instruction" (Proverbs 1:7).
   - D. "What you have learned and <u>received</u> and heard and seen in me – practice these things, and The God of peace will be with you" (Philippians 4:9).

2. If you call
   - A. How do we call to God? We ask, we pray.
   - B. Don't' doubt (James 1:5-8).
   - C. "<u>Ask</u> and it will be given to you; <u>seek</u>, and you will find; knock and it will be open to you" (Matthew 7:7).

3. If you seek
   - A. "But <u>seek</u> first the kingdom of God and his righteousness, and all these things will be added to you" (Mathew 6:33).
   - B. "And without faith it is impossible to please him, for whoever would draw near to God must

believe that he exists and that he rewards those who <u>seek</u> him" (Hebrews 11:6).

4. You will understand and find knowledge.
    A.   God gives us wisdom and understanding.
    B.   "His divine power has granted to us all things that pertain to life and godliness, through the knowledge of him who called us to his own glory and excellence," (2 Peter 2:3).
    C.   Read Proverbs 2:6–12.

CONCLUSION:

Wisdom comes from God and He is willing to give us wisdom through His word and life. If we will receive it, but we must ask for it and seek it. When we receive wisdom, we will be blessed with understanding and have a shield of faith for us to walk with through life with integrity.

Chapter 8

The Lord's Table Sermonette's

WORSHIP in the New Testament must be "acceptable" (1 Peter 2:5; Hebrews 12:28). There are 5 areas or acts of worship.

1. Singing (James 5:13; Ephesians 5:19-20; Colossians 3:16; Matthew 26:30).
2. Praying (James 5:13; Philippians 4:6).
3. Preaching (2 Timothy 4:2; Acts 20:7).
4. Giving (1 Corinthians 16:2; 2 Corinthians 9:6-7).
5. Lord's communion (Matthew 26:26-30; Acts 20:7; 1 Corinthians 11:17-34).

Every Sunday we are to partake of the Lord's communion. When a man presides over the communion he is to help the congregation think about Jesus and remember Jesus' sacrifice. We are also to be mindful of our dedication and commitment to Jesus. Below are a few ideas to talk about during the communion.

TITLE: The Tree
TEXT: Genesis 2:16-17

PURPOSE STATEMENT:
The Bible starts eternal life with a tree.

The Bible ends eternal life with a tree (the cross), but it wasn't the tree that gave Adam and Eve eternal life. Nor is it the cross that gives us eternal life. It's what was hanging from the tree. The Fruit (in Adam's case), but for us it was Jesus Christ that hung from the tree.

TITLE: Melchizedek
TEXT: Genesis 14:18-20

PURPOSE STATEMENT:
Melchizedek is like Jesus.

1. He's a king.
2. He's the priest.
3. He presides over the bread and the wine.
4. He receives an offering (tithe).
5. We do all these things today.

TITLE: Remember Jesus is our Salvation
TEXT: Acts 13:26-39

1. The message was sent.
2. The rulers did not recognize Jesus.
3. Pontus pilot executed him.
4. They took Jesus off the tree and laid Him in the tomb.
5. There were witnesses.
6. Jesus was raised.
7. The message: forgiveness of sins is through Him.
8. Through Him we are freed from the law.

TITLE: Rooted in Him
TEXT: Colossians 2:6–7

PURPOSE STATEMENT:
If we have received Christ, let us be rooted in him.

Roots dig deep. Roots are consistently growing. Roots are strong.

Where are we? Have we received Jesus? Are we digging deep in Jesus? Are we consistently growing? Are we strong?

TITLE: Remembering Jesus
TEXT: Matthew 26:6-13

PURPOSE STATEMENT:
Jesus did a beautiful thing for us.

1. The woman did something beautiful (vs 10).
2. Prepared for burial (vs.12).
3. Be told in memory (vs 13).

Jesus prepared a way to be buried with Him.
We remember Him on the first day of the week.

TITLE: Jesus Sat Down.
TEXT: "So then the Lord Jesus, after he had spoken to them, was taken up into heaven and sat down at the right hand of God" (Mark 16:19).

In the old covenant, the priests didn't sit down in the temple to show their work was never done.

Jesus sat down. Why did Jesus sit down at the right hand of the father? To show His work was done.

TITLE: Lord's Supper
TEXT: Matthew 26:26-30

The bread- Jesus' body.
The fruit of the vine- Jesus' blood is for the forgiveness of sins.
They sung a hymn (Matthew 26:30).

TITLE: Examine yourself.
TEXT: 1 Corinthians 11:23-29

Let us examine ourselves as we worship God by partaking of the bread and the fruit of the vine representing Jesus' body. Cornelius gave generously (Acts 10:1-4).

Chapter 9

Sermons from the Gospels

TITLE: The Sending of God
TEXT: Matthew 28:18-20

PURPOSE STATEMENT:
All Authority belongs to Jesus.

INTRODUCTION :

Jesus has the authority or the power to rule over the world. Everything is under the will and command of Jesus Christ.

1. Prerogative
    A. This means if you are of royal blood, especially if you are king or queen, you have certain privileges and powers. Like powers to appoint ministers and powers to remove ministers (even the prime minister) from office.
    B. Jesus came to earth with royal prerogative. He even became King!
    C. Jesus is God. (Colossians 2:9-10; Philippians 2:5-11).
    D. He was made lower than the angels (Hebrews 2:9).
    E. Jesus said His kingdom is not of this world and He has ministers/servants (John 18:36).
2. Power
    A. He had the power to exercise certain rights of appointment, or to remove certain rights. He made disciples, He healed people, and He cast out demons (Mark 2:1-13).

B. Jesus shows that He is a provider, He is Jehovah Jirah (John 2:1-11).

C. Jesus disciplined people as they turned the temple into a place of business (John 2:13-16).

D. Jesus prophesied. He also had power over death (John 2:18-22).

E. "Those who are well have no need of a physician, but those who are sick. I came not to call the righteous, but the sinners." (Mark 2:17).

F. "The Son of Man is Lord even on the Sabbath" (Mark 2:28). The Lord has power.

G. What prophet or religion can say this about their savior?

3. Purpose
A. The purpose of Jesus was to reconcile us back to God.

B. Jesus came to do God's will (Hebrews 10:7).

C. The reason Jesus Christ came as a human being, and suffered, was because He is the source and founder of salvation and created everything. (Hebrews 2:10-11, John 1:1-4, Colossians 1:18).

D. Unity, to bring people together (John 17:20-23; Ephesians 2:11-22; 1 Peter 2:5-9).

E. As Jesus calls us "through the Gospel" (2 Thessalonians 2:14), He is calling us through the good message, through His death, burial and resurrection, according to Romans 6:3-6.

F. His purpose was to give us a mission (Matthew 28:19-20).

CONCLUSION:

If we go, and make more disciples by His authority, He will be with us. This is His promise.

.

TITLE: Opportunity
TEXT: John 4:1-42

PURPOSE STATEMENT:
God will give us opportunity.

INTRODUCTION:

Opportunities are all around us. We must be open and ready to take them.

Define opportunity.

1. Jesus and the Journey
    A. Jesus was tired.
    B. He was Hungry.
    C. He was Thirsty.
    D. He was human and understands our needs.
    E. He still gave someone an opportunity, He took time out to talk to the Samaritan woman. Food is to do the will of God (John 4:31-34).

2. Samaritan Socialization
    A. Samaritans, women, strangers (All of these were looked down upon). Jesus still wanted to reach them.
    B. Poor people

3. Teaching and Training
    A. Marriage (16-18)
        i. Luke 16; Matt. 5, and 19:9
    B. Worship (20-24)
        i. True hearts for the Lord.
            Luke 10 and 17
    C. The Messiah 25-26
        i. She drops what she is doing and tells the world!

CONCLUSION:

Look at the results (39-42)! Jesus went to Samaria and stayed there!

Look at the people's response! Jesus remembered them in Acts 1:8, Acts 8. The people of Samaria accepted the Gospel!

We need to teach, and give someone an opportunity!

TITLE: Overcome
TEXT: John 16:33

PURPOSE STATEMENT:
You shall overcome the world.

INTRODUCTION:

1. Peace
   - A. A state of tranquility, of safety, of salvation
   - B. Peace is in Christ.
   - C. John 14:27, and John 16:33
   - D. Romans 14:17-19

2. Tribulation
   - A. Means: pressing, distress, stress
   - B. Distress is in the world.
   - C. Peace is not in the world. (Luke 12:51)
   - D. Matthew 24:9
   - E. Romans 2:9

Here is what Jesus was talking about: "Behold, the hour is coming, indeed it has come, when you will be scattered, each to his own home and will leave me alone. Yet I am not alone, for the Father is with me." (John 16:32) (Matthew 26:55-56 The disciples fled).

3. Overcome the world!
   - A. Overcomes means victory, which means to conquer!
   - B. John 1:5; Romans 12:21; 1 John 2:13, 4:4, and 5:4

CONCLUSION:

Overcome the world! Jesus did and you can in Christ!

112

TITLE: High Priestly Prayer
TEXT: John 17 (whole chapter)

PURPOSE STATEMENT:
Jesus could have prayed about anything.

INTRODUCTION:

Jesus was just finishing the last supper, or the communion. In the presence of His disciples he prayed out loud to God. He prayed to God on his behalf, then for His disciples who were present, and finally, He prayed for us.

1. "Glorify your Son that the Son my glorify you" (John 17:1-8)
   A. Jesus spoke in third person because He was still teaching His disciples.
   B. He had "accomplished" the will of God (Fulfilled the law) (John 17:4).
   C. "With the glory I had with you before the world existed" (John 17:5). This is Jesus' eternal nature.
   D. Notice how Jesus addressed God the Father in this prayer. When we pray, we should start our prayer addressed to God the Father and end the prayer "in Jesus' name".

2. "I am praying for them" (John 17:9-19)
   A. Jesus prayed for His disciples.
   B. He prayed for their faithfulness. He gave them His word.
   C. The world has hated them.
   D. Sanctify them in truth=set them apart for the truth, like a mission.
   E. What is truth (John 17:17)?

3. "I do not ask for these only, but also for those who will believe in me through their word" (John 17:20).
   A. Jesus prayed for us (we believe because of the teachings from the disciples).

113

B.   Jesus prayed about one thing for us (unity).
    i.   That we may be one (John 17:21).
    ii.   That we be one (John 17:22).
    iii.   That we become perfectly one (John 17:23).
C.   Why does Jesus want us to be one?
    i.   "So that the world may believe that you have sent me" (John 17:21).
    ii.   "So that the world may know that you sent me" (John 17:23).
D.   Jesus wants us to see Him in heaven. (John 17:24). Jesus will continue to make God's name known to man (John 17:26).

CONCLUSION:

We see that Jesus prayed for us and that we would be united. He never wanted so many different churches. He also doesn't want us to quarrel among ourselves. The world is watching us, if we are not unified and as one body of Christ, then the world will not believe in God. Let us be one in Christ.

TITLE: Crucify Jesus
TEXT: John 18:20-19:22

PURPOSE STATEMENT:
I find no guilt in Him.

INTRODUCTION:

Pontus Pilate really sought to release Jesus. Let us observe what happened to Jesus from the view of Pontus Pilate.

1. Pilate stated "take him yourselves and judge him" (John 18:31).
   - A. But the Jews said it was unlawful for them to kill Jesus (according to Roman law).
   - B. This got Pilate's attention. He didn't understand why Jesus needed to die.

I find no guilt in Jesus

2. Pilate asked Jesus "Are you the King of the Jews?" (John 18:32-38).
   - A. Jesus wouldn't answer.
   - B. Pilate asked what Jesus had done wrong.
   - C. Jesus tells Pilate about His Kingdom.
   - D. Jesus states I came to "bear witness to the truth".

I find no guilt in Jesus

3. "I find no guilt in him" (John 18:38-19:3).
   - A. Pilate offered the angry crowd an option to release Jesus or a real murderer or thief.
   - B. He beat Jesus. Perhaps to appease the crowd.
   - C. Then said, "That you may know I find no guilt in Him" (John 19:4).

I find no guilt in Jesus

4. Pilate frustrated with Jesus (John 19:8).
    A.   Pilate was afraid.
    B.   Pilate was frustrated.
    C.   Jesus reminded Pilate only had authority because God allowed him to have authority.

I find no guilt in Jesus

CONCLUSION:

Do you find any guilt in Jesus? The real question is "Does Jesus find guilt in you?" The guilt can be washed away. When you are baptized into Christ, you don't have any guilt.

TITLE: The Kingdom Come
TEXT: Matthew 3:2

PURPOSE STATEMENT:
The church of Christ is the Kingdom of God on earth.

INTRODUCTION:

Jesus promised the coming of His Kingdom.

1. The Kingdom is near.
    A.   Matthew 3:2
    B.   Matthew 4:17

2. Jesus promised to build His church.
    A.   Matthew 16:13-19
    B.   He gave Peter the keys.

3. The fulfillment of the Kingdom's establishment.
    A.   Instructions for the disciples. (Acts 1:8)
    B.   Acts 2:4-5 - Location and all nations present (Fulfillment of Isaiah 2:2-4).
    C.   Peter preached, (he unlocked the door to the Kingdom) (Acts 2:14-40) and people were "added" (Acts 2:41).
    D.   Acts 2:42-47- Fellowship and growth of the Kingdom followed.

CONCLUSION:

The Kingdom belongs to Jesus. The Church belongs to Jesus. We should always give God the glory and respect the Kingdom on earth, the church.

Chapter 10

Sermons from Acts

The book of Acts is known as the Acts of the Apostles. This book is a written record of what happened after Jesus was raised from the dead and after Jesus went to heaven. We should look to the book of Acts to find our restoration, our practice and our aim as New Testament Christians.

TITLE: The Gospel
TEXT: Acts 2:22-24

Purpose Statement:
The Gospel is real.

INTRODUCTION:

Acts chapter 2 is the hub of the Bible. Everything before Acts chapter 2, points to Acts chapter 2. Everything after Acts chapter 2, points back to Acts chapter 2.

1. Jesus attested to by God.
        A.   The Gospel of John has many signs that Jesus did, so that we might believe (John 20:31, 21:25).
        B.   So many signs (John 21:25).

2. You delivered/crucified him.
        A.   The people wanted Jesus to die instead of a murder Barabbas. (Mark 15:11)

3. God raised him.

A. Jesus rose on the first day of the week and left an empty tomb (John 20:1-2, 19).

CONCLUSION:

The gospel is the death, burial and resurrection (1 Corinthians 15:1-4). The response of the people (Acts 2:38). The Bible says those who **received** the word were baptized.

What will you do?

TITLE: Outside the Gate
TEXT: Acts 16:11-15

PURPOSE STATEMENT:
We need to go outside the gate.

INTRODUCTION:

Paul was willing to preach everywhere. He sought after opportunities and even made opportunities.

1. In the city (Acts 16:11-12).
    A. The city is where people are. Paul started there.
    B. Sometimes the city is more comfortable.
    C. The city may have better protection (inside the gate).

2. Outside the gate (Acts 16:13).
    A. Paul went outside the gate.
    B. Outside the gate may be a long way away from the city.
    C. Outside the gate may be dangerous.
    D. Why? Because he thought people might be outside the gate praying.

3. People outside the Gate (Acts 16:14-15).
    A. Paul found women there.
    B. The Lord opened her heart. That means we need to be reading scriptures with people.
    C. Scriptures open the hearts of people.
    D. She was baptized. She showed hospitality and thankfulness.

CONCLUSION:

We need to go outside the gate. That means we need to reach people around us and far away. We need to make sacrifices and have courage because there are people who want to do the right thing, but need help reading the scriptures.

TITLE: Paul Taught on The Sabbath Day
TEXT: Acts 18:4

PURPOSE STATEMENT:
Paul reasoned on the Sabbath day.

INTRODUCTION:

The Sabbath day is Saturday, the last day of the week.

1. Jesus Kept the Sabbath
    - A. Matthew 5:17-18. Jesus was going to fulfill the whole law perfectly.
    - B. Until Jesus fulfilled the law, the Sabbath day remained.
    - C. Jesus sat down at the right hand of God, because He fulfilled the law (Hebrews 10:12).

2. Paul taught on the Sabbath
    - A. Acts 13, 14, 16, 17 and 18 Paul taught on the Sabbath day. Why?
    - B. To reason with and persuade the Sabbath day keepers.
    - C. Paul was teaching them about Jesus and a new covenant.

3. Christians are to worship on Sunday
    - A. Jesus rose on the first day of the week. (John 20:1)
    - B. The Lord's Day Jesus didn't condemn them for meeting together, He blessed them. (John 20:1)
    - C. Paul and the Christians met on the first day of the week (Acts 20:7; 1 Corinthians 16:2).

CONCLUSION:

We are under the new covenant and must follow God's instructions in that covenant.

Chapter 11

Sermons from the Epistles

The Epistles are letters written to churches or to people in the New Testament. Paul was the worldwide missionary at that time and started or visited most of the congregations, so it only makes sense that Paul would write most of the letters.

The epistles give churches or individuals instructions, corrections or encouragement. We can learn how to be better Christians and how congregations should be conducting themselves in worship and unity and benevolence.

TITLE: Your Circle of Influence
TEXT: 2 Corinthians 10:7-18

PURPOSE STATEMENT:
To convince and convict you to study the Bible with someone else this year.

INTRODUCTION:

The purpose statement of 2 Corinthians is found in 2 Corinthians 2:9. We need to take a test of Christianity. Are we teaching others?

The outline for the book of 2 Corinthians is: chapters 1-7 (follow up from the first letter), chapters 8-9 (giving), chapters 10-13 (Paul defends his apostleship). Read 2 Corinthians 10:7-18.

We need to define two terms.

- Boast- meaning to glory in or talk about and think about all the time.

- Area of influence or sphere or measure of the rule or province- This is the area, your area of activity, interest, or expertise where you affect the behavior of other people.

1. What is it? 2 Corinthians 10:13
   A. Our Assignment

2. How does it work? 2 Corinthians 10:15
   A. Faith and influence, a symbiotic relationship.
      i. Faith increases = Influence increases
      ii. Think: "How can I hold people in my circle longer!"
      iii. Civility. 1 Corinthians 13, Abide/Agape keeps people.

3. Why does this matter? 2 Corinthians 10:16
   A. Our purpose: We are Jars of clay in for His workmanship (2 Cor. 4:7).
   B. Our commandment: Matthew 28:19-20; Mark 16:15-16; 2 Timothy 2:2
   C. Opportunity. Extend the spiritual boarders of the Kingdom of God.
   D. Because you were given a chance, pay it forward.

CONCLUSION:

There are about 2 million members of the Church of Christ in the world. If every single one of us teaches one person the Gospel every year, and that person teaches someone else every year, in 13 years we can teach 7.5 billion people (the entire world)!

TITLE: Aim for Restoration
TEXT: 2 Corinthians 13:11

PURPOSE STATEMENT:
Let's Aim for restoration

INTRODUCTION :

In the English Standard Version Bible, the word used is restoration.

1. Restoration
   A. Means to return something to its former or original place.
   B. "Your restoration is what we pray for" (2 Corinthians 13:9).

2. Reconciliation
   A. Galatians 6:1. Restoration brings us closer to God, closer to each other.
   B. Hebrews 13:19

3. Redemption
   A. Restoration brings us redemption (1 Peter 5:10).

CONCLUSION:

Restoration is associated with reconciliation and redemption. Let's be restorers. That's what God expects.

TITLE: Singing to God
TEXT: Ephesians 5:19-20

PURPOSE STATEMENT:
God tells us how to worship Him.

INTRODUCTION:

Read Ephesians 5:19-20/Colossians 3:16

Let's ask ourselves why?

1. New Covenant
   A. Under the old covenant priests conducted the worship 2 Chronicles 29:24-25. They played instruments and sacrificed animals.
   B. Jeremiah 31:31
      i. Write it on their hearts.
      ii. Singing with your heart.
      iii. Hebrews 10:1 - Old covenant a shadow.

   C. New covenant, old covenant is done away (Heb. 8:13).
      i. The old had regulations, so does the new covenant (Heb. 9:1).

2. Holy Priests
   A. Acceptable worship (1 Peter 2:5; Hebrews 12:28).
   B. The priests of every covenant participate in worship according to God's regulation, not according to their own regulation.
3. Spirit and truth
   A. Worship God in spirit and truth (John 4:23).
   B. Spirit is the right attitude.
   C. Truth is God's word. (John 17:17)

CONCLUSION:

The Bible commands us to sing in the New Testament. The Bible commanded the use of certain instruments in the Old Testament. Therefore, because God's word is the Bible, we know exactly what God wants us to do in the New Testament, sing without instruments.

TITLE: Women in the church
TEXT: 1 Timothy 2:8-15

PURPOSE STATEMENT:
To explain the role of women in the church.

INTRODUCTION:

Everyone is important, but God made us different. Even nature will tell you that a man cannot be pregnant with a baby. However, nature shows us that a woman can be pregnant. Even in the church God has designated roles for men and women.

1. Respectable
   A. Respectable apparel. Respectful behavior (Titus 2:3).
   B. Modesty, not costly attire. Don't show off.
   C. Self-control (1 Timothy 2:9). Respectful and pure conduct (1 Peter 3:2).
   D. If women are not respectable, their husbands can't serve as elders or deacons (1 Timothy 3:11).

2. Submissive/Quiet
   A. Are not to teach over a man (1 Timothy 2:12).
   B. Are not to exercise authority over a man (1 Timothy 2:12).
   C. She is to remain quiet (1 Timothy 2:11; 1 Peter 3:4).
   D. Wives be subject to your husbands (1 Peter 3:1; 3:5; Ephesians 5:22-23).
   E. Women are not permitted to teach in a congregation (1 Corinthians 14:33-37).
   F. They are permitted to sing. Ephesians 5:19 is about the entire congregation addressing one another.

3. Older women teaching women and children.

A. Older women are to teach younger women (Titus 2:3-4).
B. They are to love children and husband.
C. Have good works (1 Timothy 2:10).

CONCLUSION:

Why does the Bible tell women they have this role? "So that the word of God may not be reviled" (Titus 2:5). Adam was formed first and it was the woman who was deceived. Therefore, a women's role supersedes all cultures as this is an issue from the beginning of time (1 Timothy 2:13-14).

TITLE: Men in the Church
TEXT: 1 Timothy 2:8

PURPOSE STATEMENT:
Men have responsibilities to God, their family and the church.

INTRODUCTION:

Men are to be leading their families to church and leading the church.

1. Responsibility to God
   - A. Men should be praying to God (1 Timothy 2:8).
   - B. Young men-self-control, good works, integrity, sound speech (Titus 2:6-8).
   - C. Older men-sober minded, self-controlled, and steadfast.

2. Responsibility to family
   - A. Show honor and understanding to your wife (1 Peter 3:7).
   - B. Love your wife, protect her, cherish her (Ephesians 5:25, 28, 31, 33).
   - C. Fathers are to lead their children in an honorable way and discipline them (Ephesians 6:4).

3. Responsibility to the church
   - A. Qualifications for elders, must be men (1 Timothy 3:1-7; Titus 2:1-2).
   - B. Qualifications for deacons, must be men (1 Timothy 3:8-13).
   - C. Men are to lead the church in prayer, singing, preaching, and presiding over the Lord's communion and leadership roles.

CONCLUSION:

When men are living righteously before God, they will bring their family with them to the Lord and worship God together as a family. Men have responsibilities. That is the way God designed.

TITLE: Inexpressible and Unspeakable Joy
TEXT: 1 Peter 1:8-9

PURPOSE STATEMENT:
We can have inexpressible joy!

INTRODUCTION :

The perfect house, the perfect car. Does it have joy? We should have Joy, we are Christians! Understand that Peter wrote during difficult circumstances. We all have difficult circumstances from time to time. He wrote during Nero's persecution. How can we have inexpressible joy during difficult circumstances?

1. Love
    A. "We love because he first loved us" (1John 4:19). This love is an endearing love. To love deeply.
    B. We love Jesus because of what he did for us!
    C. Even Paul said that these three abide, faith, hope and love and the greatest is love (1 Corinthians 13:13).
    D. Love is the ingredient to inexpressible joy, prior to the ingredient believe.

2. Believe
    A. "Believe" means a deep seeded trust and confidence.
    B. "And without faith it is impossible to please him, for whoever would draw near to God must believe that he exists and that he rewards those how seek him" (Hebrews 11:6).
    C. Thomas said, "Unless I see in his hands the mark of nails and place my hand into his side, I will never believe" (John 20:25).
    D. Jesus said, "Have you believed because you have seen me? Blessed are those who have not seen and yet have believed" (John 20:29).

131

    E.   You will be rewarded for believing in Jesus in this way.

    F.   You believe what he did (died for you) but even more you believe and even love what he is doing. He is your mediator, your high priest and that he is coming back to take you to heaven!

3. Rejoice

    A.   Rejoice means to rejoice and to extol greatly.

    B.   Joy means gladness and delight.

    C.   Rejoice with Gladness and delight that is unspeakable or inexpressible.

    D.   We are unable to communicate how glad and delighted we are because our joy is glory filled!

    E.   Glory = that is full with incredible dignity and excellence.

CONCLUSION:

When you're having a bad day, you must Love, Believe and Rejoice. When you're having a good day, you must Love, Believe and Rejoice!

Why? Because God Loved you first! Because you love him dearly, because you have total confidence in him, because you will obtain the outcome of your faith, salvation for your souls." **The result of your inexpressible, unspeakable Joy that is glory filled is salvation for your soul!**

You have a soul that wants to be forgiven, that wants to be set free, a soul that has a beacon calling it back to the home of the soul. Give into your Spirit and release the Joy God has given that is glory filled!

Love, Believe, Rejoice, Salvation.

TITLE: Holiness
TEXT: 1 Peter 1:15-17

Purpose Statement:
Are you Holy?

INTRODUCTION:

Definition- "To Be Holy". Holy means "set apart for a God, morally and spiritually excellent."

1. God's presence is Holy
    A. God's name Holy. "My name is Holy" says the Lord. (Ezekiel 39:7)
    B. God's person is holy (Isaiah 6:3).
    C. God's presence is Holy (Exodus 3:4-6). (Read the burning bush story). Moses was to stand on Holy ground. Why was the ground Holy? Because God's presence was there.

2. God's People are Holy
    A. God can make a people, a group of people, holy (Deuteronomy 7:6).
    B. Because God loves them (Deuteronomy 7:7-11) (Notice the privilege of holiness came with expectations of obedience).
    C. God's people are people and people have problems. So how do we get along as a group of people and be Holy together? Read Colossians 3:12-17. Collectively individuals are referred to as "holy ones." Therefore, Holy ones must put into practice these qualities.
    D. How a people aren't holy, read Isaiah 6:4-13, the unworthiness of Isaiah and a people who weren't Holy.

3. You are Holy
    A. Our commandment: 1 Peter 1:15-17

    B.   Bring holiness to completion, this is how (2 Corinthians 7:1).

    C.   Psalms 119:9, Guard your heart with the word of God.

CONCLUSION

We as Christians need to be Holy, set apart for God, on a mission to spread the truth, love, joy and even holiness to the world.

TITLE: Alpha and Omega
TEXT: Revelation 1:8

PURPOSE STATEMENT:
Jesus is the beginning and is the end.

INTRODUCTION:

Jesus had no beginning and He has no end. Jesus is eternal. He also has been and always will be.

1. Who was-
   A. Alpha - the beginning (John 1:1-3).
   B. Created everything (Colossians 1:15-17; Genesis 1:26). ("Let us" make man, after "Our") (Genesis 1:26).
   C. His existence before He was man.
      i. Genesis 18:1
      ii. "I am Sent you" (Exodus 3:2), "Before Abraham was, I am" (John 8:58).
      iii. "And all drank the same spiritual drink, for they drank from the spiritual rock that followed them, and the rock was Christ" (1 Corinthians 10:4).
      iv. Who spoke to Moses face to face (Exodus 33:11)?

2. Who is-
   A. Jesus became a human (Philippians 2:5-8).
   B. Jesus was a young man who grew in wisdom, stature, and favor of God and Man (Luke 2:52).
   C. Jesus' ministry- fed thousands, healed many people, performed many wonders, works and miracles. "Now there are also many other things that Jesus did. Were every one of them to be written, I suppose that the world itself could not contain the books that would be written" (John 21:25).

135

D. Died, Buried, resurrected
E. Serves now as High Priest and mediator for us.
F. He is "The way, the truth and the life" (John 14:6).

3. Who is to come-
   A. Omega- Jesus is the last.
   B. The end of sin and death (for some). The beginning of eternity for others (heaven).
   C. He has gone to prepare a room, a place in heaven, and is coming back (John 14:2).
   D. Isaiah 41:4, and 44:6
   E. 1 Thessalonians 4:16-18.

CONCLUSION:

The Lord is, was and will always be. He is eternal.

Chapter 12

Biographical Sermons & Funeral Sermons

TITLE: Rahab
TEXT: Joshua 2

PURPOSE STATEMENT:
A woman of great faith, is a woman of action.

INTRODUCTION:

What does it mean to be a great woman? What does the Bible show us?

1. Rahab's understanding
   A. She heard what the Lord did.
   B. She heard what the people of God did.

2. Rahab's confession
   A. When she heard, her heart melted.
   B. She had a fearful respect of God and His people.
   C. "Your God, He is God." Her confession.
   D. Acts 8:37-38 The Ethiopian believed with his heart, confessed and followed with action.

3. Rahab's action
   A. Her action is already decided when she secured the spies.
   B. She reminded them that she had dealt kindly with them.

C. She protected what she believed was good.
D. She protected their secret, even after they left.

4. Rahab's expectation
  A. She asked for redemption not only for herself, not only for her parents, but her whole household.
  B. She tied a scarlet cord in her window that she was instructed to do.
  C. She stayed in her house. Rahab and her household was saved.

CONCLUSION:

Great women have great faith followed by great action. Great women have great expectations followed by blessings from God.

Rahab was the mother of Boaz who fathered Obed, who fathered Jesse who fathered David and Jesus came from that lineage. She is mentioned in Hebrews 11:31.

TITLE: Where You Lead I Will Follow
TEXT: Ruth 1:16-17

PURPOSE STATEMENT:
Where you Lead me, I will follow.

INTRODUCTION:

How are we leading people?

1. Your God shall be my God.
   - A.   She had an opportunity to go back to her home and worship her gods.

2. Your people shall be my people (Church).
   - A.   She found a new people.

3. Where you lodge, I will lodge (Home).
   - A.   She was willing to sleep on the floor.
   - B.   She was willing to work for just the crumbs, the left overs.

4. Where you go I will go (City).
   - A.   She was willing to go to a place she did not know.
   - B.   She was willing to move.

CONCLUSION:

Where God leads us, I will go. If he takes me to a city that I don't like I will follow. If he gives me a job I don't like I'll work it.

TITLE: An Extraordinary Woman
TEXT: Luke 2:36-38

PURPOSE STATEMENT:
What an extraordinary woman!

INTRODUCTION:

The word ordinary means normal or expected. Extraordinary means outside of normal. Therefore, this could mean something really great or it may mean something strange. In this case it means something really great!

1. Her sorrow (Luke 2:36-37)
   A. Anna was a virgin and then married. Her husband died and she remained a widow for a long time.
   B. The tribe she came from, Asher, had a bad reputation. They were unfaithful to God. Therefore, people thought she had a bad reputation.
   C. Because she was without family, she was alone.

2. Her Character (Luke 2:37)
   A. It is during these tough times our true character is revealed. How do we act when we are struggling? How do we act when we are alone? God knows all things.
   B. Anna was faithful to God!
   C. She worshiped daily, prayed daily, and fasted daily. The Bibles says she prayed even at night!
   D. She did not depart from the temple.

3. Her Joy (Luke 2:38)
   A. "Coming up that very hour". What hour was that? (Luke 2:22-32)
   B. Because Anna was always at the temple worshiping God and praying to God, she saw Jesus!

C. She also heard what Simon said about Jesus (a light to the Gentiles and salvation).
D. She gave thanks to God!
E. She spoke to everyone about the salvation of Jerusalem!

CONCLUSION

What an extraordinary woman!

We all have struggles from time to time. May we have good character, and worship God. May we pray to God every day and gather together with His church.

May God bless you.

Death and dying

This section is difficult. It's difficult to comfort people and their families during times of departure. Isaiah says "The Lord has given me the tongue of those who are taught, that I may know how to sustain with a word him who is weary" (Isaiah 50:4).

TITLE: No Tears in Heaven
TEXT: Isaiah 24:8-9

Purpose statement:
There are no tears in heaven!

Introduction: Death, pain and difficulties befall all of us.

1. God will take away death.
2. He will wipe away tears from all faces.
3. If we wait for him he will save us.

CONCLUSION:

Let us be glad and rejoice in His salvation. Death is not destruction, but is departure for a Christian. We may have tears, but our loved one does not.

TITLE: Life Is Short
TEXT: Hebrews 9:27

PURPOSE STATEMENT:
To help you prepare for life after death.

INTRODUCTION:

How quickly do our children grow up? How about our life? How long do we really have on this earth?

1. Life is Short
      A.   Job 14:1
      B.   Hebrews 9:27
      C.   James 4:13-16

2. We must be prepared
      A.   Ephesians 2:10
      B.   Colossians 3:17
      C.   How do we prepare?
            i.   Romans 6:3-4

CONCLUSION:

Psalms 116:15 and Rev. 2:10. Finally let us examine 1 Corinthians 15:53-57.

Appendix

Dear Brethren,

In light of the fact that there are some current prevailing issues which concern the fellowship of churches of Christ, many affecting changes within our brotherhood, I wish to address some of these issues briefly and my relationship to them. Whether I'm on the mission field, or preaching here stateside, below are doctrines you can expect to hear from me. While the list below does not address every doctrine, it addresses major doctrines that are very important.

1. I believe in the inspiration, authority, and inerrancy of Holy Scripture (2 Timothy 3:16, 17). I reject the postmodern view that it is not possible to discern and ascertain the truth of the scripture.

2. I believe in the one Church that belongs to Christ and is His body (Ephesians 1:22, 23 and 4:4).

3. I believe that the saved are in that body for which Jesus died and that He is the Savior of only of those who are in the body, the church (Acts 2:47, 20:28; Ephesians 5:23).

4. I believe that baptism is for the remission of sins and is essential to one's salvation (Mark 16:16; Acts 2:38; 1Peter 3:21).

5. Because I respect the silence of the scriptures as well as its pronouncements, I believe that a-cappella is the only accept-able form of music in collective Christian worship. To teach, promote, or condone the use of instrumental music would go beyond what the word teaches and would

fail to respect its silence (Ephesians 5:19; Colossians 3:16; 2 John 9).

6. I do not believe that women can teach over a man, nor can a woman have an open, public and active leadership role in Christian worship where men are present (1 Timothy 2:11, 12, 1 Corinthians 14:33–35).

--- Chad Garrett

What is God's Prescription to remedy our sins?

Do you believe in God's authority?

Yes?

No?

GOD'S REMEDY
Romans 5:8
Matthew 26:28
2 Corinthians 5:21
1 Peter 1:18-19

What is man's biggest problem?

SIN
1 John 3:4
Romans 3:23
Isaiah 59:2
Romans 6:23

Separation from God.
Genesis 3

2 Timothy 3:16-17
Hebrews 3:4
Who built these things?
It is logical to believe in a designer/creator?

Fulfilled Prophecy:
Isaiah 44:28 & 45:1
Amos 8:9
Matthew 27:45

SCIENCE-
Job 26:7
(Earth hangs)
Isaiah 40:22
(Circle of Earth)
Psalms 8:8
(Fish paths of sea)
Genesis 17:11
Leviticus 12:3
(medical clotting)

FAITH/BELIEF
Romans 10:17
John 8:24
Hebrews 11:6

REPENT
Luke 13:3 & 5
Acts 17:30
2 Peter 3:9
1 Corinthians 10:9

CONFESS
Matthew 10:32-33
Romans 10:9-10
Acts 8:37

BAPTISM
Mark 16:16
Acts 2:38
1 Peter 3:21

You are FORGIVEN!

"And now why do you wait? Rise and be baptized and wash away your sins, calling on his name." Acts 22: 16

What about baptism?

Sprinkling vs. Burial
Romans 6:3-4 Acts 8:38
Colossians 2:12
Previous Baptism
Acts 19:1-5
Ephesians 4:5
Where Baptism Puts You:
Acts 2:41 & 47
Galatians 3:26-27

IN CHRIST'S CHURCH!

CHRIST'S Church

Colossians 1:18
How Many Bodies?
Matthew 16:18
Ephesians 4:4-6
Commitment to Christ's Church
Matthew 13:3-8,18-23
Matthew 6:33 Luke 9:62
Matthew 10:37

Living in CHRIST

All Spiritual Blessings- Ephesians 1:3
Redemption-Ephesians 1:7
Eternal Life- 1 John 5:11
Salvation- 2 Timothy 2:10
New Creature-2 Corinthians 5:17
No Condemnation-Romans 8:1

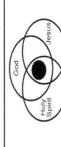

49272894R00087

Made in the USA
Columbia, SC
20 January 2019